LA BELLE EPOQUE
236 S. E. 10th TERRACE
FT. LAUDERDALE, FL 33301
(305) 463-0881

BRONZES
SCULPTORS & FOUNDERS

—Frontispiece

3143. "LYS"—Bust
Austrian. Circa: 1890
Porcelain: Green glaze and
Gold matte. Height: 14"
Manufacturer: Ernst Wahliss/
Turn-Wien (Vienna)

Right—

3144. "ALICE"—Nymph
           of the Valley
By Pittaluga
Italian. Circa: 1890
White Carrara marble
Height: 42" Width: 19½"
Depth: 11"

VOLUME
IV

ABAGE ENCYCLOPEDIA

BRONZES
SCULPTORS & FOUNDERS
1800-1930

by HAROLD BERMAN

ABAGE/Publishers
Chicago, Illinois

FIRST EDITION

Abage Publishers

6430 N. Western Ave., Chicago, Illinois 60645

Library of Congress Catalog Card Number: 74-78612

Printed in the United States of America

ACKNOWLEDGEMENTS

Our most sincere thank you to everyone who helped us along the way to finishing this four volume encyclopedia. An equally sincere appology to those who we have inadvertently forgotten to include here. Many others we have elected not to mention to protect their privacy.

In Paris we thank J. Chardon et Petits-Fils Founders for their generous gifts of files and old catalogs. Pierre Retrouve, Foundry Du Marais for teaching me the scorching art of sand casting. The Grossman's, Anne Paree Parfum Co. for good advice and restaurants. My guide Simon Benaiche for getting me here to there and through red taped doors.

No one helped more than Martin Steinfeld in New York—two weeks of photographing, information and shared lunches. Also, Universe Antiques, Madison Galleries, Lanchart Antiques, Renee Antiques, Inc., Bronz' Art Antiques, Robert E. Mann Antiques and Palace Antiques.

Again in Volume IV we thank Stanley Hirsch for his many hours of help in preparing two sections of Collection Francaise sculptures.

Thanks to Al and Sharane of Incolay Studios for unvaulting their unique, company bronze/ivory collection.

Our thanks to Ira Bartfield, coordinator of photography at the National Gallery of Art, Washington D.C. and to Walter Aberth of Aberth-Szymanski, Fine Arts for their generous contributions.

In Beverly Hills, on Canon Drive, several Nouveau-Deco galleries—We've misplaced their cards, please forgive us. Shadow Hills Antiques gave us much to include. California is great!

On the Antique/Exposition circuit our friends and generous donors: Powderhorn Antiques, Jim Sullivan Antiques, Louis Ryan Antiques, Bob Harris Weaponry, Luse & D'Auito Antiques, Antiques by Beth and Edmondo, Hickman's Antiques, J. Allison Antiques, Bryant Antiques, H. Brooks Antiques, Gene and Gwen, S.R.B. Fine Antiques, McLeod and D'Orazio—Clock Tower Gallery, Century Antiques, Platinum Alley, Joella's House, Mark Gallery, Casal's Antiques, Ken McBride, Barbara Saks Antiques, Ada's Treasures, Custer Investment Co., Interiors Unlimited, Newport Trading Co., Joyce Wilkie Antiques. Weber Antique Gal.

Close to home: Campanile Galleries, Inc., Art Bronzes Co., Prestige Galleries, Flamingo, Howard Art Galleries, Kodner Galleries, River Road Antiques—Alton, Old World Antiques.

These wonderful individuals helped us for the first time or again in Volume IV: V.B. Skul, O.H. Priller, M.M. Bauer, M.C. West, J.H. Brooks, M.P.J. Tishman, F. Bezak, R. Ciatelli, J. Stern, L. Sable, C. Newsom, R. Conklin, P.E. Lessek, V. Bacon II, R. Benson, T.A. Baker, E. Brown, Dr. Brown, E. D'Amico, R.C.I. Reynolds, M. Crabtree, G. Rosenberg, B.C. Smith, F. D'Amato, R. Thornton, R. Stewart, A. Coleman, S. Torrisi, A. Weiner, B. Marshfield, M. Hubay, M. Blank, A. Morlock, L.B. Katz, W. Burger, A.N. Cutler, A. Duncan, M. Fraser, R. Ellison, W.R. Plunkett, W. Porges, A. Conforti, J.C. Redfern, P.J. Pierce, A. Ernsten, H.A. Silverstein, P.J. Nagoda, W.B. Weinberg, L. Morgan, T. Zaydon, G. Lundeen, F. Christ, Y.B. Johnson. Thank you, Thank you.

Continued from Acknowledgements in Volume III.

UNCERTAIN BEGINNING

An alternative to collecting statuary from the past is choosing the right new limited-editions as investments in the future.

During 1979 the above plate was offered to the public. To the best of our knowledge it was the first executed within the age-old tradition of bronze-ivory art.

Produced by Fonderíe Incolay, a division of Incolay Studios, Inc., San Fernando, California, this plate is a fresh re-interpretation by American artist/sculptor James Warren Roberts of Georges Omèrth's bronze-ivory figurines. "Uncertain Beginning" is the first in Life's Interludes, a four-plate limited annual edition series.

CONTENTS

VOLUME FOUR

ART NOUVEAU
By Victor H. Bacon II

THE flowering of Art Nouveau began in the 1880's and came to an end in the early 1900's. Although short lived, the movement continues until this day to fascinate, mystify and give flight to dreams of fancy.

A dichotomy, however, existed among the artists of the day that separated them both aesthetically and philosophically. Individual expression among the artists of the Period was far from uniform. There were no inveterate patterns, preconceived limitations, or inviolable motifs. Some envisioned Art Nouveau as the light and inspiration of the future —others saw the movement as a degenerate and abased statement of blatant sexuality.

Before long this revolutionary approach descended to an uncontrolled chaotic, artistic melee. A style with so many names: Jugendstil, Style Liberty, Le Style Moderne, Sezession, Arte Modernista, Tiffany Style, could only be tenuously structured and end, as it did, in a confused state—but what a marvelous confusion!

Amongst the philosophic and stylistic groups that gave rise to, and were part of, the Period were the Pre-Raphaelite Brotherhood and the Symbolists. More than any of the fragmented groups making up the Art Nouveau Period, they contributed most poignantly to what is now recognized as the Art Nouveau Style.

Pre-Raphaelites: Dante, Rossetti, Burne-Jones, Charles Lowther, etc., sought to explore fundamental mysticism through techniques and thematic artistic restrictions of the late Renaissance and unabashedly included certain popular motifs of the period suffusing heroines and subjects with seductive qualities unknown to their exalted predecessors, creating an unequal yoke between men and women.

3147. NYMPH OF THE FIELDS
By Pittaluga
Italy. c1890. Carrara marble. Ht: 66¼"
Photo reproduced by courtesy of the
National Gallery of Art, Washington D.C.

Symbolists: Munch, Boldini, Von
   Stuck, Walter Sauer and others
attempted to provide a manifesto of
decadence and psychological intro-
spection co-mingled with a certain
ephemeral beauty. The time, by all
indications was right for Art
Nouveau. The dehumanizing indus-
trial Revolution had for many,
reached intolerable limits. Artists
reacted violently. Nature, and
above all woman, became the subject
artists viewed as untainted by the
new mechanized culture infringing
upon them.

Touchstones of the style were
   flowers, undulating organic forms,
and primordial effulgence—graceful,
fresh, and dangerous. Woman, a favorite theme, was seen as the living
embodiment of beauty with long flowing tresses falling around further
folds and curves. The Art Nouveau
"Femme" confronted her viewer as a
willing, ambitious partner. A sen-
suous hide-and-seek was aroused between artwork and observer. Inher-
ent in the work was a promise of
fugitive romance—dark and silent.

A break from the traditional concept
   of woman increased as time went on.
An inscrutable image of woman became
increasingly inviting and perverse.
There was no escape from the sensual-
ity of nature; nor was an attempt
made to minimize the suggestiveness
of long floral blossoming buds, con-
voluted sea shells and tentacled
marine life.

The Art Nouveau woman, her innocence
   threatened by all that was about
her, appeared alternately defenseless,
passive or welcoming. As seen in the
works of Vibert Gustave Michel, Louis
Chalon, George Coudray, Pittaluga and
others, she was caught up in orgiastic
nature, inevitably succumbing to it;
there was little doubt that although
strong, woman would ultimately give
way to the natural force of her
creation.

3148. NYMPH OF THE WOODS
     By Pittaluga
Italy. c1890. Carrara marble. Ht: 66½"
Photo reproduced by courtesy of the
National Gallery of Art, Washington D.C.

FOUNDERS
Keyed to the Photographic Section

A. B. Paris. Seal#17 4098

A.G. Paris. Seal#62,42 3435

A.R. Vienna. Seal#58 3380 3547 367A 367B 3894
3901 3971 3983 4009 4015 4201

B.D. Vrai Bronze Paris. Seal#18 3493 4426

B.S. Austria. 3542

B.W. Ecthe Bronce Berlin. 3295

Barbedienne, Ferdinand Paris. Seal#6
3349 3361 3409 3429 3431 3451 3721 4062 4155
4160 4179 4182 4223 4225 4353 4378 4415 4460
4495 4514 4785 4786 4828

Bellair, R. & Co. Berlin. Seal#34 3363

Bentejacs Bordeaux. 3772

Bergman Vienna. Seal#77 3584 3586 3600 4778

Berndorf Foundry Austria. 3944

Bierling, Guss. Dresden. 4396

Bingen et Costenoble Paris. 4864

Bisset Paris. 4824

Bisson & Ribot Fabricants-Editeurs Paris. 4497

Blanchet, H. Paris. 3701

Blot, Eugène Paris. Seal#51,68 3789

Boileau, Henri Paris. 4089

Bonnard, Henry Bronze Co., N.Y. 4383

Bransch, V.R. Bildbuss Hamburg. 3499

Bronze Garante Seal#40 4050

Bronze Garanti Seal#41 3411 4475

Bronze Garanti Au Titre, France. 3821

Chardon, J. et Petit Fils Paris. (Active)
4452 4647 4648 4651

Chirazzi, Fonderie Napoli. 3620

Chopin Volhynia. Pol-Rus. border 3553

Christofle & Cie. Paris. 4528 4529

Colin, E. & Cie. Paris. 3654 3796 3866 3929
4283 4408 4412 4455 4865

Colin, Maison Paris. 4037

Cottin, R. Paris. 4779

Delafontaine, A. D. Paris. 4131

Delafontaine et Saulo Paris. 4395

Deniere a Paris. 3723

Deutsche Echte-Bronze. 3235

Duplan et Salles Bronziers Paris. 4031 4032

E.N. Germany. 4554

Ehberger, A.C.E. & Co. 3631

Etch Bronze Berlin. 4507

Etling-Paris. 3986 4017 4547 4644 4645 4657

F. P. Napoli. 3688

Fabrication Francaise Paris. Seal#20
3294 3518 4061 4074

Fiat-Lux, V.F. Paris. 4361

Finzel Berlin. 3498

Franklin Mint U.S.A. 3684 3685

Friedenau Berlin. 4270

Friedrichshagen Berlin. 4758

Gadaix Paris. 4385

Gauthier, Ch. Paris. Seal#79 3804 3828

Gertz, Abling v. Bild. Berlin. 3242

Gladenbeck Echte Bronce Garanti Berlin.
3365 3375 3417 3421

Gladenbeck-Friedrich & Shoger Berlin. 3501

Gladenbeck, Oskar & Sohn Berlin. Seal#48
3262 3381 3385 3456 3641 3699 3959 4556 4794

Gladenbeck, W.P. v. Guss. Berlin. 4575

Goldscheider Paris. Seal#38,43 3920 4500

Gorham New York. 3624 3625 3626 3627 3628
3629 4244

Grandhomme Paris. 4078

Griffoul Newark, New Jersey. 4746

Grönig, Franz Berlin. 3441

Guillemard, Marcel Paris. 4171

H. V. Bronze D'Art Paris. 3305 3485

Haase-Hsbg. Hesburg. 3268

Heinze, G. Guss. Berlin. 3511

Hirsch, J. B. Co. Brooklyn, N.Y. Seal#81
(Active) 3160-3208 and 4680-4740

Hohwiller Paris. 3946

K. B. Echte Bronze München. 3508

Keyserzinn-Pewter Germany. 3902

Konforti, Gino Florence. 3680

Krass, Ernst Berlin. 4020 4021 4295

Krohne, B. Berlin. 4187

Kunst-Erziessere, Wien. 3700

Kunst Foundry New York. 4570

L. N. & J. L. Paris. Seal#44 3686

L. V. Bronze Garanti Seal#22   3758 3793 3806
  4115 4521

LaPointe Paris.   4413

Lastele Paris. Seal#55   4583

Lauchhammer Bildguss Köln.   4205 4784

LeVerrier de Paris. Seal#61   4589

Linz, Ch. v. Guss. Nbg. Nuremburg.   3679

Louchet & Cie. Paris.   3832 3858 3882 3885
  4364

Luppens, H. Brüxelles. Seal#37   3823

M. B. F. Echte Bronze   3251

M. B. V. Echte-Bronce Köln.   3467

Marinelli Fdry. Florence. (Active) 4741

Mazet, H. Paris.   4649

McGann, T. F. & Sons Co. U.S.A.   3702

Medalic Art Co. Danbury, Conn. (Active) 3307

Menard, André Fondeur Paris.   3352

Miroy Frères a Paris.   4449

Montoy Editeurs Paris.   3492

Mottheau Paris.   4613

N. B. W. Echte Bronze Berlin.   3245

N. W. Germany.   4559

Nissel & Siroka Wien.   3612

Noack, H. Friedenaw Berlin.   4557

Offenhausen Berlin.   3543

P. L. Köln.   3277

P. Y. Vienna.   3353

Pandiani, A. Milano.   3561 3562 3563 3566

Peyrol Fondeur Paris.   3368

Piltzing, Martin v. Berlin. Seal#82
  3414 4399

Pinedo, E. Paris. Seals#23, 91   4520

Preiss/Kassler (P.K.) Berlin.   4653

Quesnel, E. Paris.   3313

R. H. B. Werk St. Bildguss Germany. 4512

R. K. Bronze Garanti Germany.   4508

Rehberger, A. C. & Co. Chicago.   4849

Rochard Paris.   3638

Roman Bronze Works New York.   326B 3703 3708
  3709 4194 4247 4569 4571 4753 4756 4771

Rudier, Alexis Paris.   4841

S. P. A. Colinet (monogram seal)   4674

S. K. Echte Bronze Baveria.   3297

Sachs, Robert Bronze Warenfabrik Berlin.
  3440

Salesio Fondeur Paris.   4877

Sanson, F. P. Succr. Hamburg. Seal#3   3274

Schaffer & Walcker Köln.   3259

Shtange, N. St. Petersburg.   3560

Siot-Decauville Paris. Seals#24, 71
  3281 3340 3503 3607 3862 3883 4391 4404 4408
  4409 4499 4614

Société des Bronzes de Paris. Seal#8
  3261 3269 3271 3428 3466 3538 3639 3652 3762
  3767 3770 3774 3778 3787 3788 3790 3826 4044
  4344 4428 4368

Starr, Theodore B. Inc. U.S.A.   3877

Susse Frères Paris. Seals#12, 72-Lost wax
  3444 3445 3487 3711 3732 3809 3860 4162 4238
  4354 4453 4532 4585 4588 4615 4616 4831 4832

Tassel, E. Fondeur Paris.   3646 4390

Thiébaut Frères Paris. Seals#9, 39   3315 3915

Tiptoz Bronzier Paris.   4530

Ulrich, U. Vienna.   3573

Union de Maitres Sculpteurs Paris. Seal#88
  4355

Valsuani Paris. Seals#67, 67A   3306 3308

Venturi Arte Fdry. Bologna. (Active)   4742

Vignali, G. Firenze Milano.   3660 4192

Viguali Firenze, Roma.   4092

Volz, W. München.   3384

Vrai Bronze Garanti Paris. Seal#27 3222 3243
  4525

Vrai Bronze Seal#28 4304

Weston, Dell Fdry. U.S.A. (Active) 4757

Wiener-Kanstwerkstättes Brandel Berlin.   3520

Woerffel, C. E. St. Petersburg.   3545 3552

Seal#84 3797   Seal#87 4186   Seal#89, 90 4403

Bronze Sculptures
PHOTOGRAPHIC SECTION

Caption information is presented in the following sequence:

- Number and title of sculpture, actual or descriptive.
- Sculptor and (born-died) or estimated years worked (Wk: c)
- Country of origin (the bronze)

- Year cast or estimate (c)
- Colors or patina (Pt:)
- Height in inches (Ht:)
- Seal number (seal index)
- Founder and city (Fdr:)

Additional information is given when pertinent and of interest—as room permits. See Forenote to indices.

3158. AT THE BATH
Unsigned/unmarked
Amer. c1930. Pt: Dark brown. Ht: 18"
Twelve angles (30' X 12 = 360')
Motorized turntable synchronized to
automatic Minolta 35MM SRT-101. Lens
used: f=135MM Tele Rokkor. Kodak Pan-
atomic X film, ASA 35. Photo lab used
throughout four volume set, "ABAGE".

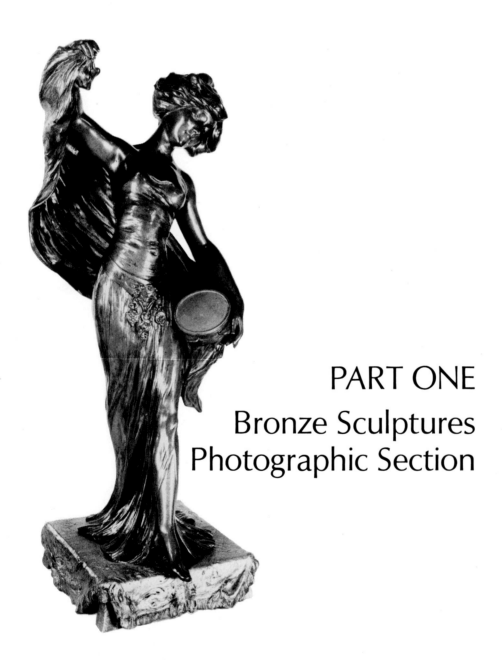

PART ONE
Bronze Sculptures
Photographic Section

COLLECTION FRANCAISE

The discovery of the priceless moulds of the Collection Francaise is a fascinating story of the rescue of hidden art treasure. It spanned the period of two World Wars and three generations of the Hirsch Foundry. (See Vol. III - Pgs. 789-796)

One must understand methods of casting in order to appreciate the importance and value of these moulds. Unlike sand-casting and lost-wax methods of casting bronze, where the moulds are "wasted" (consumed) and must be re-made for each casting, the Collection Francaise moulds are permanent and can be used again and again. To be faithful to the sculptor's artistry and achieve life-like detail, the moulds are made in many sections which are re-assembled after each casting.

3160. CHEVAUX MARINS   by Emile Picault
c1887   Ht: 24"

3161. JEANNE D'ARC VICTORIEUSE   by Doriot
c1865   Ht: 25"

During World War II, in order to protect the moulds from pillage, hundreds of moulds comprising thousands of these intricate sections were buried in the cellars of the original French foundries. After the war, the search, which resembled an archaelogical expedition, went on year after year. Gradually, these invaluable moulds were unearthed by members of the Hirsch family who had special knowledge of their whereabouts.

Thousands of mould sections for more than 200 subjects were shipped from Paris to the Hirsch foundry in New York over a period of 15 years. It required ten months to assemble some 1800 sections for the 120 moulds that made the first 12 complete subjects. Over 100 additional subjects were assembled in the years that followed. There are many sections and moulds yet to be identified — a mountainous three-dimensional puzzle, the solving of which has gone on for thirty years and will, no doubt, continue for many more.

Continued on page 840

3162

3163

3164

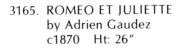

3165

3166

3167

3165. ROMEO ET JULIETTE
by Adrien Gaudez
c1870   Ht: 26"

3162. CONQUE MARINE
by Emile Picault
c1875   Ht: 18"

3163. LES PECHEURS
by L. F. Moreau
c1870   Ht: 20"

3164. LE COQ
by Melolle
c1898   Ht: 18"

3166-7 BEAU TEMPS
by Auguste Moreau
c1880   Hts: 18½"

3168. LES MUSICIENNES
by L. F. Moreau
c1885   Ht: 15"

3171-2 LA FILLE FRANCAISE
by L. F. Moreau
c1876   Hts: 24"

3173. LA RENCONTRE
by Auguste Moreau
c1875   Ht: 23"

3169-70 ANCIEN CAVALIER
by C. Desmeure
c1883   Hts: 10½"

3174. CONFIDENCE
by L. F. Moreau
c1880   Ht: 17″

3175. SYLPHIDE
by Mathurin Moreau
c1875   Ht: 20½″

3176-7. ROMEO—JULIETTE
by Adrien Gaudez
c1870   Hts: 23″

3178. BUIRE
by Hippolyte Moreau
c1889   Ht: 27½″

3180

3181

3179

3182

3183

3179. LES MUSES
by Ruisseau
c1871   Ht: 25½"

3180. A LA PLUS BELLE
by Auguste Moreau
c1865   Ht: 16"

3181. ETUDE MUSICALE
by L. F. Moreau
c1875   Ht: 16"

3182-3 PRINTEMPS
by E. Bruchon
c1890   Hts: 23" & 28"

3184   3185

3186

3187

3188

3189

3190

3184-5. LES MUSICIENNES
    by L. F. Moreau
    c1880   Hts: 13"

3186-7. LE GENIE COURONNE
    by L. F. Moreau
    c1881   Hts: 21"

3188. PAN
    by Auguste Moreau
    c1889   Ht: 30"

3189-90. AU PRESSOIR—FANEUSE
    by L. F. Moreau
    c1885   Hts: 14"

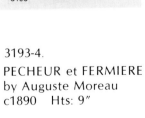

3195-6.
GLORIFICATION
by Levisseur
c1899   Hts: 18½"

3193-4.
PECHEUR et FERMIERE
by Auguste Moreau
c1890   Hts: 9"

3191-2 DANSEUSE et DANSEUR
NAPOLITAIN
by C. Anfrie
c1885   Hts: 17½" & 16½"

3197. LE GENIE COURONNE
by L. F. Moreau
c1881   Ht: 27"

3198. FONTAINE ET RUISSEAU
by Auguste Moreau
c1885   Ht: 15"

3199. FILLE AU CHAT
by Eutrope Bouret
c1885   Ht: 23"

3200. CUPIDON
by Auguste Moreau
c1875   Ht: 28½"

The Collection Francaise is cast in spelter which is also known as *French Bronze*. The illustrated subjects (3160-3202) are either in current production or will be within the next ten years. Collection Francaise subjects are illustrated on Pages 789-796 of Volume III and on Page 841 of this volume.

The discovery and preservation of this treasure of XIX Century French sculpture is truly as remarkable as the J. B. Hirsch foundry itself, the last remaining foundry of its kind in the world.

3201. LA PETITE ANGE
by L. F. Moreau
c1870   Ht: 22½"

3202. LA PETITE ANGE
by L. F. Moreau
c1870   Ht: 18½"
Shown with milifiore globe

3202

3204

3205

3206

3207

3208

CONTEMPORARY

These bronzed, spelter figurines will be cast from the original French molds. As American issues, they are positively identified by the Collection Francaise seal with *fleur-de-lis* motif.

3203-4. LA RENCONTRE—Chance Encounter
By Auguste Moreau   Wk: c1860-1910
France.   c1875.   Pt: Brown.   Ht: 22″   Seal #81
Fdr: J.B. Hirsch Co., Brooklyn, N.Y.

3205-6. DÉFENSE DU FOYER—Father-Son
By Robert Bouillot   Wk: c1890-1925
France.   c1900.   Pt: Brown.   Hts: 15½″, 14½″
Fdr: J.B. Hirsch Co., N.Y.   Seal #81

3207-8. FÊTE DU PRINTEMPS—Spring Festival
By Louis Hottot   (1834-1905)
France.   c1890.   Pt: Brown.   Ht: 21″   Seal #81
Fdr: J.B. Hirsch Co., Brooklyn, N.Y.

3209

3210

3211

3212

3209. PARIS SPORT   by F. Etienne Leroux   (1836-1906)
France.   c1890.   Pt: Shades of brown.   Ht: 13″

3210. FIELD HOCKEY   by Franz Iffland   Wk: c1885-1915
Germany.   c1910.   Pt: Black.   Ht: 10″

3211. ATHLETE   by C. Anfrie   Wk: c1880-1915
France.   c1910.   Pt: Dark brown.   Ht: 16″

3212. THE RUNNER   by Emile Raissiguier   (1851-1932)
France.   Dated: 1886.   Pt: Light brown.   Ht: 24″

3213. BEFORE THE GAME Illegible signature
France.   c1920.   Pt: Green-brown.   Ht: 13½″

3214. THE KEGLER   Unsigned work
Germany.   c1920.   Pt: Yellow-brown.   Ht: 7½″

3215. THE PASS   by Schmidt-Hofer   Wk: c1900-1925
Germany.   c1920.   Pt: Dark green.   Ht: 10″

3216. FOOTBALL U.S.A.   Unsigned work
America.   Dated: 1934.   Pt: Brown.   Ht: 6½″

3217. THE BOWLER   by H. Scholter
Germany.   c1930.   Pt: Dark brown.   Ht: 8″

3218. SHOT-PUTTER   by Rudolf Kaesbach   b1873
Germany.   c1910.   Pt: Gray-brown.   Ht: 6″

3213

3214

3216

3215

321B

3217

3218

321B. DEUX SOUS DERNIER BOUQUET
By Eutrope Bouret (1833-1906)
France. c1885. Pt: Green and brown. Hts: 8″ & 12″
Honorable mention at Paris, Salon des Beaux Arts.

3219

3220

3221

3222

3223

844

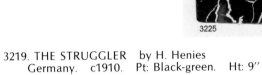

3226   3227

3228

3219. THE STRUGGLER   by H. Henies
    Germany.   c1910.   Pt: Black-green.   Ht: 9"

3220. LE LUTTEUR   by Ernst Seger   b1868-
    Germany.   c1900.   Pt: Brown.   Ht: 12"
Conserved: Wallraf-Richartz Museum, Cologne.

3221. THE DIGGER   by Hugo Kaufmann   (1868-1919)
    Germany.   Dated: 1919.   Pt: Dark brown.   Ht: 18½"

3222. THE DIGGER   by Jean Garnier   Wk: c1885-1910
    France.   c1905.   Pt: Brown.   Ht: 8½"   Seal #27
Won honorable mention in Paris Salon of 1892.

3223. BRUTE SLEDGE   by H. Bayer-Schulte
    Germany.   c1910.   Pt: Black.   Ht: 11½"

3224. THE HEWN LOG   by Otto Stichling   (1866-1912)
    Germany.   c1905.   Pt: Dark green.   Ht: 12"

3225. THE STONE MASON   Unsigned work
    Germany.   c1915.   Pt: Yellow-brown.   Ht: 7"

3226-7. FOUNDRY WORKERS   Monogram on bases
    Germany.   c1910.   Pt: Brown,   Hts: 6½" & 6"

3228. THE BURDEN   Ludwig Kowalczewski   Wk: c1890-1910
    Germany.   c1900.   Pt: Dark brown.   Ht: 11½"

3229

3230

3231

3232

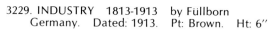

3233

3229. INDUSTRY   1813-1913   by Füllborn
   Germany.   Dated: 1913.   Pt: Brown.   Ht: 6″

3230. BLACKSMITH MASTER   Unsigned work
   Germany.   c1910.   Pt: Gray-brown.   Ht: 6½″

3231. BLACKSMITH   by G. Deihle
   Germany.   c1910.   Pt: Gray-brown.   Ht: 9½″

3232. APPRENTICE GEARMAKER   Unsigned
   Germany.   c1910.   Pt: Light brown.   Ht: 4″

3233. BRICKLAYER   by Schmidt-Hofer   Wk: c1900-1925
   Germany.   c1920.   Pt: Red-brown.   Ht: 12″

3234. HEIMKEHR—HOMEWARD   Fdr: Gladenbeck
   Germany.   c1925.   Pt: Dark green.   Ht: 8½″

3235. HOMEWARD BOUND   by F. Brandt
   Germany.   c1920.   Pt: Brown.   Ht: 16″
   Fdr.: Deutsche, Echte-Bronze

3236. HOMEWARD BOUND II   by F. Brandt
   Germany.   c1925.   Pt: Brown-green.   Ht: 19½″

3237. MILL WORKER   by Bretislav Benda   b1897-
   Czech.   1925.   Pt: Green-brown.   Ht: 16″

3238. THE LABORER   by Gamboge   Seal #41
   France.   c1910.   Pt: Brown-green.   Ht: 14″

3239. END OF DAY   Unsigned work
   Austria.   c1915.   Pt: Dark brown.   Ht: 11½″

3234

3235

3236

3237

3238

3239

847

3241

3242

3241. MINER   by Jacob Plessner   b1871-
   Germany.   c1915.   Pt: Green-brown.   Ht: 14"

3242. MINER   Illegible signature
   Germany.   c1920.   Pt: Gray-black.   Ht: 21"
Fdr: Abling u. Gertz Bild., Berlin.

3240

3240. MINER   by E. Beck
   Wk: c1890-1925
   Germany.   c1905.
   Pt: Dark green.   Ht: 17"

3244. YOUNG MINER   by Raphael Hubert   b1884-
   France.   c1915.   Pt: Brown tones.   Ht: 9½"

3245. YOUNG MINER   by Schmidt-Felling   Wk: c1895-1930
   Germany.   c1915.   Pt: Dark brown.   Ht: 9"
Fdr: N.B.W., Echte Bronze, Berlin.

3246. MINERS   by Adolph Kissner
   Luxemburg.   c1920.   Pt: Gray-black.   Ht: 12½"
Bronze was originally centered on large marble dish.

848

3243

3244

3245

3246

3243. MINER   by Oscar Bastian   b1847-
Swiss.   c1900.   Pt: Brown.   Ht: 7″
Seal #27

3248

3249

ARBEITER GIESSEREI
Foundry Worker

3247. FOUNDRY WORKER
   By Gerhard A. Janensch   b1860-
Germany.   c1915.   Pt: Brown.   Ht: 10½″
Won Gold Medal in Berlin, 1892.
Note glove on left hand.

3248. FOUNDRY WORKER   by Schaffert
   Germany.   c1915.   Pt: Dark brown.   Ht: 12½″

3249. FOUNDRY WORKER   by Richard W. Lange
   Germany.   Dated: 1924.   Pt: Brown.   Ht: 7½″

3247

3250

3251

3252

3250. ARBEITER GIESSEREI
By G. Adolf Janensch   b1860-
Germany.   Dated: 1918.   Pt: Brown.   Ht: 11″

3252. FOUNDRY WORKER
By Georges Morin   b1874-
Germany.   c1910.   Pt: Tones of brown.   Ht: 12½″

3251. FOUNDER   by Schmelenberg
Germany.   c1920.   Pt: Black-brown.   Ht: 10″
Fdr: M.B.F. Echte Bronze.   Note rag on rod.

3255. RAIL MAKER
   By Schmidt-Felling   Wk: c1895-1930
Germany.   c1905.   Pt: Black-green.   Ht: 19½″

3254. RAIL MAKER
   By Reinhard Schnauder   (1856-1923)
Germany.   c1900.   Pt: Brown.   Ht: 24½″

3256

3257

3258

3259

3256. RAIL MAKER   Illegible signature
Germany.   c1900.   Pt: Brown-green.   Ht: 15"

3257. RAIL MAKER
By Schmidt-Felling   Wk: c1895-1930
Germany.   c1905.   Pt: Black.   Ht: 15"

3258. MILL WORKER   by V. Funk
Germany.   c1920.   Pt: Dark brown.   Ht: 18½"

3259. INGOT AND TONGS
By Friedrich J. Reusch   (1843-1906)
Germany.   Dated: 1896.   Pt: Ylo-brown.   Ht: 11½"
Fdr: A.C., Schaffer & Walcker, Köln.

3262. ARBEIT KRÖNT
    By Martin Götze   b1865-
Germany.   c1900.   Pt: Black.   Ht: 21″
Fdr: Akt.-Ges: Gladenbeck, Berlin.

3261. GLOIRE AU TRAVAIL
    By Henri Levasseur   b1853-
France.   c1900.   Pt: Black.   Ht: 45″   Seal #8
Fdr: Société des Bronzes de Paris. Other editions of 36″, 29″, 21″

ARBEIT KRÖNT
The crowning glory of work — a
symbolic reward for the laborer.

3263. ARBEIT KRÖNT
    By Martin Goetze/Götze b1865-
Germany. c1910. Pt: Brown. Ht: 10½″

3265. ARBEIT KRÖNT
    By Martin Götze b1865-
Germany. Dated: 1906. Pt: Black. Ht: 19″

3266

3267

3268

326A

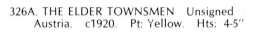

326A. THE ELDER TOWNSMEN Unsigned
Austria. c1920. Pt: Yellow. Hts: 4-5"

326B

326B. POE by Edith Woodman Burroughs (1871-1916)
America. Dated: 1909. Pt: Brown. Circ: 7"
Fdr: Roman Bronze Works, New York.

3266. SLEDGEMAN   by E. Greier   Wk: c1900-1915
   Germany.   c1910.   Pt: Brown-green.   Ht: 9½''

3267. THE MILLWRIGHT
   By P. L. Kowalczewski   Wk: c1890-1910
Germany.   c1900.   Pt: Brown tones.   Ht: 16½''

3268. L'MARTELEUR
   By Constantin Meunier   (1831-1905)
Belgium.   c1890.   Pt: Black.   Ht: 15½''
Fdr: H. Haase-Hsbg (Hesburg)

3269. MARTELEUR   by Henri Levasseur   b1853-
   France.   c1895.   Pt: Yellow-brown.   Seal #8
Fdr: Société des Bronzes. Editions: 13'', 18'', 24'', 33''

3271. LES PUDDLEURS   by Henri Levasseur   b1853-
   France.   c1895.   Pt: Brown.   Seal #8
Fdr: Société des Bronzes. Editions: 19'', 25'', 34''
Kneeling figure was not offered solo.

3274. LABOR (Hors Concours)
    By Adrien Etienne Gaudez   (1845-1902)
France.   c1890.   Pt: Gray-black.   Ht: 17'',, 24'', 31''
Fdr: F.P. Sanson Succr., Hamburg.   Seal #3

3273. LE FORGERON
    By Eugène-Ernest Chrétien   (1840-1909)
France.   c1885.   Pt: Dark brown.   Ht: 28''
Retailer: Tiffany & Co., New York.
See Annabel Lee, Volume II, #1155

3275. BLACKSMITH   by F. Gass
Ger.   Dated: 1919.   Pt: Green-brown.   Ht: 16½″

3277. BLACKSMITH
     By Gotthilf Jaeger   b1871-
Germany.   c1920.   Pt: Dark brown.   Ht: 13½″, 24½″
Monogram: P.L. Köln (Cologne).
Name is commonly mistaken for Faeger/Faegen.

3277

3279. LE FER—THE IRON WORKER
By Emile-Louis Picault   b1839-
France.   c1890.   Pt: Green-brown.   Ht: 16″, 24″, 30″

3281. L'FORGERON
By Alfred Boucher   (1850-1934)
France.   c1920.   Pt: Light brown.   Ht: 31″   Seal #24
Fdr: Siot-Decauville Fondeur Editeur, 24, Boulevard des
Capucines (showrooms). Telephone 118-10 — in 1921.

3282

3283

3284

3285

3286

3282. PAUSING SMITH   Unsigned
    Germany.   c1920.   Pt: Brown.   Ht: 9"

3283. PAUSING SMITH
    By E. Saalmann   Wk: c1918-1932
Germany.   c1920.   Pt: Brown.   Ht: 9½"

3284. WORKING SMITH   Illegible
    Germany.   c1920.   Pt: Brown-green.   Ht: 8½"

3285. WORKING SMITH   by F. Jensen
    Germany.   c1920.   Pt: Gray-brown.   Ht: 11"

3286. RESTING SMITH   by E. Zago (Italian)
    France.   c1910.   Dark brown.   Ht: 7½"

3287. LE DROIT CIVIQUE
By Maurice (Mce) Constant Wk: c1890-1913
France. c1900. Pt: Black Ht: 7½″, 14″, 23″, *30″*
Retailer: Casa Bella Artes, Buenos Aires.

3288. DEVOIR CIVIQUE
By Eugène Marioton b1854-
France. c1900. Pt: Brown. Ht: 16″, 21″, *30″*

3289

3290

3291

3292

3293

3294

3289. BLACKSMITH
    By Heinz Müller   b1872-
Ger. c1910.   Pt: Ylo-brn. Ht: c10''

3290. THE HORSE SHOER
    By E. Beck   Wk: c1890-1925
Ger. c1910.   Brown. Ht: 9''

3291. PLANNED WORK
    By E. Beck   Wk: c1890-1925
Ger. c1910.   Pt: Grn-brn. Ht: 7''

3292. LE FER
    By Mce. Constant   Wk: c1890-1913
France. c1900. Pt: Green. Ht: 7½''
Compare to #3287: anvil/book, sword/
hammer, calipers on base. Edited in
larger sizes to 30''.

3293. BLACKSMITH
    By Schmidt-Felling   Wk: c1895-1930
Ger. c1918. Pt. Black. Ht: 14''

3294. FORGERON
    By Etienne-Henri Dumaige   (1830-1888)
Fr. c1880. Brown. Ht: 31'' Seal #20
Fabrication Francaise, Paris. W.M.

3295

3296

3297

3298

3295. STEEL CONSTRUCTION
By Schmidt-Felling   Wk: c1895-1930
Germany.   c1920.   Pt: Dark brown.   Ht: c12"
Fdr: B.W. Ecthe Bronce, Berlin.

3296. BRIDGE WORKER   by Schaffert   Wk: c1900-1913
Germany.   c1910.   Pt: Dark brown.   Ht: 13½"

3297. BLACKSMITH   by Schmidt-Hofer   Wk: c1900-1925
Germany.   c1920.   Pt: Black.   Ht: 16", 22"
Fdr: S.K. Ecthe Bronze, Bavaria.

3298. STONE CUTTER   Illegible signature
Germany.   c1910.   Pt: Dark brown.   Ht: 11"

3299. DUTCH FISHERMEN   Unsigned work
Austria.   c1910.   Pt: Yellow-brown.   Ht: 8½"

3300. TOILING FISHERMAN   by Karl Kowalczewski   b1876-
Germany.   c1910.   Pt: Black-green.   Ht: 15"
Retailer: Sammlung, München.

3299

3300

3301

3301. NEPTUNIAN CATCH   by André F. Clemencin   b1878-
      France.   c1920.   Pt: Brown-black.   Ht: 15''
Note different behavior of the two mermaids.

3304

3305

3303

3304. SWORDMAKER—Armorer
Unsigned   White-metal
France.   c1910.   Pt: Dark brown.   Ht: 15″

3305. LE TRAVAIL
By Antoine Bofill   Wk: c1895-1925
France.   c1910.   Pt: Red-brown.   Ht: 15½″
Fdr: H.V. Bronze D'Art, Paris.
Also cast with squared base design.

3303. GLORY OF WORK
By Jöblinger
Austria.   c1900.   Pt: Black.   Ht: 15½″
Placement of hands and branch which is
reliefed on apron simplifies the
casting procedure.

3306. BULL   by Alfredo Pina   b1883-
France.   c1910.   Brown.   Ht: 16″
Fdr: Valsuani, Lost wax, Paris. Seal #67
Pina was a student-disciple of Auguste Rodin.
Valsuani did much of Rodin's bronze casting.

3306

3307

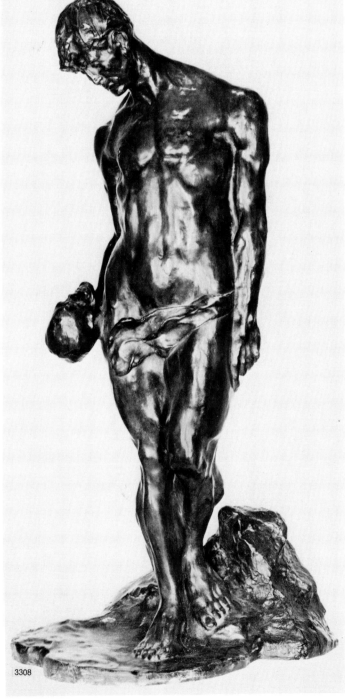

3308

3307. MOUNTAIN GOAT
    By George DuPont Pratt
Amer.   Dated: 1914.   Brown.   Ht: 7½"
Born 1869, died 1935 in New York. Goat was
cast by Medalic Art Co., Danbury Conn. First
casting in Metropolitan Museum, N.Y.

3308. ASHES TO ASHES
    By Alfredo Pina   b1883-
Fr.   c1915.   Black.   Ht: 30"   Seal #62
Fdr: Valsuani, Lost wax, Paris.

3309

3310

3311

3312

3309. SWORDMAKER—Armorer
    By Adrien-Etienne Gaudez   (1845-1902)
France.   c1885.   Pt: Brown.   Ht: 13½″

3310. PIED PIPER   by Christ v. Otto
    Ger.   Dated: 1880.   Brown.   Ht: 20″
The musician in German legend who rid
Hamelin of its rats and later its children.

3311. NUBIAN WARRIOR   by Alix Bronier
    France.   c1900.   Pt: Brown.   Ht: 14″
Note: Animal skin, long bow and quiver.

3312. 16TH CENTURY SOLDIER   by Alix Bronier
    France.   c1900.   Pt: Brown.   Ht: 14″
Germanic type, has cartridge belt with ball and
powder and wheel lock carbine.

3313

3314

3315

3313. RUSSO-MONGOLIAN SOLDIER
By Eugène Louis Lamy (1800-1890)
France. Dated: 1844. Pt: Black. Ht: 19½"
Founder: E. Quesnel, Paris.
Armor includes chainmail, pistol, flint-lock rifle, cartridge
yoke, saber and dagger.

3314. EARLY FRENCH SOLDIER
By Emile Picault b1839-
France. c1900. Pt: Brown. Ht: 18" etc.
Note: powder flask, wheel-lock carbine, sword, medallion
and leather helmet with ear-protectors.

3315. FRANCOIS VILLON
By Jean Etcheto (1853-1889)
France. 1883. Pt: Brown. Ht: 29" Seal #9
Fdr: Thiébaut Frères, Paris. Edited in several smaller and
larger sizes.
Villon was a 13th century French lyric poet.

3318. ON GUARD

By Edouard Drouot (1859-1945)
France. c1910. Pt: Black/ivory.
Ht: 14″

3317. TESTING HIS FOIL by Benedict Rougelet (1834-1894)
France. c1885. Pt: Gold-brown. Ht: 12″

3316. TESTING HIS FOIL by Benedict Rougelet (1834-1894)
France. c1885. Pt: Gold-brown. Ht: 12″

3319. FENCER AT REST
by A.J. Lavergne   Wk: c1860-1890
France.   c1885.   Pt: Dark brown.   Ht: 11″

3320. FENCER AT REST
by Adolphe-Jean Lavergne
France.   c1885.   Pt: Dark brown.   Ht: 14″

331A. TESTING HER FOIL   by Desire-Alfred Jaquet
France.   c1905.   Pt: Dark brown.   Ht: 7½″
Jaquet born in Paris, 1873. Honorable mention in
1905 Salon des Beaux Arts.

3321. PREPARING TO FENCE   by L. Madrassi   Wk: c1869-1914
France.   c1890.   Pt: Black. *15″, 31″*

3322

3323

3324

3325

3326

3327

3322. SWORD AND SHIELD   by Alfred Morét
     France.   c1880.   Pt: Black.   Ht: 7½″
Founder's monogram: M. over S.   (1853-1913)

3323. SWORD IN HAND
     By Schwalenberg   Wk: c1898-1922
Germany.   c1905.   Pt: Yellow.   Ht: 9″

3324. WAITING   by Andreas
     France.   c1910.   Pt: Dark brown.   Ht: 11½″
Coin type guarantee seal on base.

3325. WAITING   by Schmidt-Felling   Wk: c1895-1930
     Germany.   c1910.   Pt: Black.   Ht: 11½″
Echte Bronze, dye stamp on base.

3326. READY TO FIGHT   by Höffmann
     Germany.   c1910.   Pt: Green-brown.   Ht: 10″

3327. READY TO FIGHT
     By Schmidt-Felling   Wk: c1895-1930
Germany.   c1910.   Pt: Black.   Ht: 7½″

3328

3329

3330

3331

3328. SWORD AND SHIELD
    By Schwalenberg   Wk: c1898-1922
Germany.   c1905.   Pt: Light brown.   Ht: 9½″

3329. TESTING THE FOIL
    By Gotthilf Jäger   b1871-
Germany.   c1900.   Pt: Black.   Ht: 11½″

3330. TESTING THE FOIL
    By Schmidt-Felling   Wk: c1895-1930
Germany.   c1910.   Pt: Brown.   Ht: 11″

3331. THE LONG SWORD
    By Schwalenberg   Wk: c1898-1922
Germany.   c1900.   Pt: Black. Ht: 6½″
Bronce Garanti seal on base.

3332. THE SHARP BLADE
    By Alfred Morét   (1853-1913)
France.   c1890.   Pt: Ylo-brown.   Ht: 8″

3333. THE CHALLENGER
    By Füllborn   Wk: c1905-1920
Germany.   c1910.   Pt: Dark brown.
Bronce Garanti seal on base.   Ht: 8″

3332

3333

3335. SHIELD OF MEDUSA
    By C. Holand
Germany.   c1900.
Pt: Gray-brown.   Ht: 14″

3336. COMBATANT
    By Bruno Zack   Wk: c1918-1935
Germany.   c1925.   Pt: Black.   Ht: 19½″

3337. LONG THRUST
    By E. Beck   Wk: c1890-1925
Germany.   c1900.   Pt: Brown.   Ht: 11½″

3334. GERMANIC WARRIOR
    By Schmidt-Felling   Wk: 1895-1930
Germany.   c1895.   Pt. Black.   Ht: 22″, 13½″

3338. GLADIATOR
    By Richard Abraham   Wk: c1915-1935
Germany.   c1920.   Pt: Green-black.   Ht: 12″
Founder's Monogram: B.S.

3339. WOMAN WARRIOR
By Schwalenberg   Wk: c1898-1922
Germany.   c1910.   Pt: Brown.   Ht: 10″

333A. NUDE WITH DAGGER
By Rudolf Marcuse   b1878-
Germany.   c1910.   Pt: Dark brown.   Ht: c8″

3340. VINGT ANS—The Twenty Year Old
By Raoul Larche   (1860-1912)
France.   c1900.   Pt: Grn-brn.   Ht: 20½″
Fdr: Siot, Seal #24, Editions: 35″, 27½″,
20½″, 12″, 10″ Doré patina was 50% extra.

875

3342

3344

3347

3342. TEUTONIC KNIGHT
By Prof. Victor Heinrich Seifert   b1870-
Germany.   c1900.   Pt: Green, brown.   Ht: 10″, 19″, 26½″
Reduction from an unidentified monument.

3344. LE PREUR—The Crusader
By Maurice Constant   Wk: c1890-1913
France.   c1900.   Pt: Silver, gold and brown.
Ht: 12″, 15″ w/ivory, 23″, 30″   Ref: V.III   #2493.

3347. THE CRUSADER—Benediction
By Claire Jean Roberte Colinet   Wk: c1910-1940
France.   c1920.   Pt: Gold, brown/ivory.   Ht: 25½″
Personally initialled on monogrammed-seal and
numbered, as are many of this sculptor's bronze
editions.

3350

3349

3350. IN HOC SIGNO VINCES
By Reuper
France.   c1910.   Pt: Ylo-brn.
Carved ivory face.   Ht: 16″

3349. BERTRAND DUGUESCLIN
By E. Frēmiet   (1824-1910)
France. Salon: 1902.   Gold Doré.
Fdr: F. Barbedienne, Paris. 21½″
Ref: Vol. III, #2495.

3351. INVOCATION
        By Bruno Zack   Wk: c1918-1935
Germany.   Dated: 1926.   Brown.   c22″

3352. KNIGHT (French monument)
        By Jean Boucher   (1870-1939)
Fr.   1905.   Pt: Brown.   *11″, 16″, 24½″*
Fdr: Andre Ménard Fondeur, Paris.

3353. KNIGHT OF VERONA
        By Hans Müller   b1873-
Austria.   c1900.   Pt: Ylo-brn.
Ht: 17½″   Marble: 5½″ red green.
Fdr's. monogram: P.Y., Vienna.

3354

3356

3357

3354. KNIGHT—Late Medieval
    By Schmidt-Felling   Wk: c1890-1930
Germany. c1910.   Pt: Brown.   Ht: 13"
Wears *morion*, a visorless helmet.

3356. RESCUE OF UTA
    By Schmidt-Felling   Wk: c1890-1930
Germany. Dated:1910.   Pt: Brown.   Ht: 15"
Leo saves Uta from life in dark room.

3357. KNIGHT—Late Medieval
    By A. v. Strantz—Fecit
Germany. c1910.   Pt: Dark brown.   Ht: 13"
Wears *basinet* with moveable chin protector.

3359. CARABINIER
    By Mathilde Thomas   Wk: c1879-1914
France.   c1890.   Pt: Brown.   Ht: 22½"
French cavalry officer—2nd-half 19th century.

3361. MOUNTED ROYALTY
    By Emmanuel Frémiet   (1824-1910)
France.   c1885.   Pt: Brown.   Ht: 19"
Reduced from unidentified French monument.
Ferdinand Barbedienne, founder.

3363

3364

3365

3363. MOORISH SOLDIER
 By Georges Morin   b1874-
Ger.   Dated: 1910.   Pt: Brown.   Ht: 15″
Fdr: R. Bellair & Co., Berlin.   Seal #34

3364. GREEK WARRIOR
 By Rudolf Küchler   b1867-
Germany.   c1900.   Pt: Brown.   Ht: 17″
Head of Medusa on shield notched for spear.

3365. MOUNTED AMAZON
 By Richter-Wolf   b1868-
Ger.   c1910.   Br. & Bl.   Ht: 12″
Fdr: Gladenbeck, Echte Bronce Garanti.

336A. KNIGHT
 By Ferdinand Frick
Ger.   Dated: 1906.   Pt: Brown.   Ht: 14″

336A

3366

3367

3368

3366. VOW TO AVENGE
By M. Tito
Aust.   c1905.   Pt: Blue-green.   Ht: 12½″

3367. LANCER
By P. Marius Jensen   b1883-
Germany.   c1910.   Pt: Brn-blk.   Ht: 10½″

3368. UN CAVALIER ARABE
By Isadore Bonheur   (1827-1901)
France.   Salon: 1881.   Pt: Yellow.   Ht: 25″
Fdr: Peyrol. Retailer: Boudet, Paris.

3371. CHARGING AMAZON
Unsigned work
Ger.   c1925.   Pt: Brown-black.   Ht: 19″

3370. TAKING AIM
By Helmuth Schievelkamp   b1849-
Ger.   c1890.   Pt: Dark brown.   Ht: 21½″

3372. FEEDING HER MOUNT
By Helmuth Schievelkamp   b1849-
Ger.   c1890.   Pt: Gray-black.   Ht: 11″

3373. YOUNG AMAZON
By O. Hertel
Ger. c1900. Pt: Brn, blk, ylo. Ht: 6½"

3375. AMAZIONIAN FAREWELL
By Hermann Haase-Ilsenburg b1879-
Germany. c1905. Pt: Black. Ht: 15½"
Fdr: Gladenbeck, Berlin.

3376. YOUNG AMAZON by K. Delin
Germany. c1900. Pt: Blk. Ht: 9½"

885

3377

3378

3379

3380

3377. ROMAN SOLDIER   by P. Thiermann
    Germany.   Dated: 1919.   Pt: Yellow.   Ht: 15½''

3378. SHIELD AND DAGGER   by P. Thiermann
    Germany.   c1920.   Pt: Yellow.   Ht: 12''

3379. SPEARMAN—Roman   by P. Thiermann
    Germany.   c1920.   Pt: Brown.   Ht: 11½''

3380. GREEK WARRIOR   by P. Marius Jensen   b1883-
    Denmark.   c1910.   Pt: Blue-green.   Ht: 11''

3381. SPEAR AND SHIELD   by Füllborn
    Germany.   c1910.   Pt: Brown.   Ht: 8½''
Fdr: Oskar Gladenbeck. Berlin.

3382. SPEAR AND SHIELD   by Schmidt-Felling
    Germany.   c1910.   Pt: Blue-green.   Ht: 12½''

3383. ATTACKING GREEK   by Schwalenberg
    Germany.   c1920.   Pt: Brown.   Ht: 12½''

3384. ROMAN WARRIOR   by Kichut
    Germany.   c1910.   Pt: Brown.   Ht: 8½''
Fdr: W. Volz, München.

3385. GREEK WARRIOR   by P. Thiermann
    Germany.   c1920.   Pt: Brown-black.   Ht: 10''
Fdr: Oskar Gladenbeck, Berlin.

3381

3382

3383

3384

3385

3389

3388

3387

3389. SPOR-VELUCHION
By L. Eisenberger   Wk: c1895-1914
Germany.   c1900.   Pt: Brown, black.   Ht: 17½″

3388. AWAITING ORDERS
By Schmidt-Felling   Wk: c1895-1930
Germany.   c1910.   Pt: Black.   Ht: 18″

3387. BEFORE THE BATTLE
By L. Eisenberger   Wk: c1895-1914
Germany.   c1900.   Pt: Jet black.   Ht: 20½″

3390. PREPARING FOR BATTLE
    Ferdinand Lugerth   Wk: c1885-1915
Austria. 1903.   Pt: Brown-green.   Ht: 10½″
Seal #58

3391. CENTURIAN   by M. Frank
    Germany.   c1920.   Pt: Dark brown.   Ht: 9″
Ancient Roman commander of 100 men was centurian.

3392. DRESSING FOR BATTLE
    By Schmidt-Felling   Wk: c1895-1930
    Germany. c1925.   Pt: Brown.   Ht: 22″

3393

3394

3395

3396

KRIEGER RÜSTEND
German equivalent to
preparing for battle.

3393. KRIEGER RÜSTEND   Illegible signature
Germany.   c1920.   Pt: Black.   Ht: 9½"

3394. ROMAN LANCER
By Gotthilf Jaeger   b1871-
Germany.   Dated: 1913.   Pt: Brown.   Ht: 15½"

3395. BEFORE THE BATTLE
By Mathiew Molitor   (1873-1929)
Germany.   c1910.   Pt: Brown.   Ht: 10½"

3396. COURAGE—VALOR
By L. Eisenberger   Wk: c1895-1913
Germany.   1907.   Pt: Black.   Ht: 15", 22"

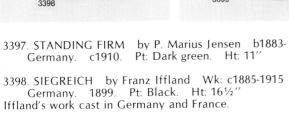

3397. STANDING FIRM   by P. Marius Jensen   b1883-
   Germany.   c1910.   Pt: Dark green.   Ht: 11″

3398. SIEGREICH   by Franz Iffland   Wk: c1885-1915
   Germany.   1899.   Pt: Black.   Ht: 16½″
Iffland's work cast in Germany and France.

3399. THE VALIANT ONE
   By E. Beck   Wk: c1890-1925
Germany.   c1912.   Pt: Black.   Ht: 14″

3400. BRIEF RESPITE
   By Schmidt-Hofer   Wk: c1895-1930
Germany.   c1910.   Dark brown.   Ht: 17″/spear

3401. JAVELIN THROWER
    By Franz Iffland   Wk: c1885-1915
Germany.   c1900.   Pt: Black.   Ht: 17½''

3402. JAVELIN THROWER
    By Schmidt-Hofer   Wk: c1900-1925
Germany.   Pt: Brown-black.   c1900.   Ht: 9½''

3403. JAVELIN THROWER
    By Karl Möbius   b1876-
Germany.   1910.   Pt: Gray-brown.   Ht: 12''

3404. LANCEUR DE JAVELOT
    By Abraham Movier
France.   Dated: 1903.   Pt: Black.   Ht: 9½''

3405. JAVELIN THROWER
    By Helmuth Schievelkamp   b1849-
Germany.   c1890.   Pt: Brown.   Ht: 8''

340A. NARCISSUS—Classical Antiquity
    Italy. 19th-20th museum reductions in various sizes. Patinas in corroded green and brown. In myth, Echo died in vain for his love. Punishment was to forever reflect upon himself in a pool.

3406. SACRIFICIAL SNAKE   by R. Palmier
    Austria.   c1910.   Pt: Brown.   Ht: 9″
Usually seen holding aloft a large snake.

3407. FLOWER OF YOUTH   Illegible signature
    Germany.   c1910.   Pt: Brown.   Ht: 13½″

3408. EXALTED YOUTH   Antiquity
    Germany.   c1900.   Pt: Brown.   Ht: 11″
Freely sculpted museum replicas of several sizes differ in facial details while remaining quite accurate in overall positioning.

3409. EXALTED YOUTH   Antiquity
    France.   c1910.   Pt: Brown.   Ht: 29½″
Fdr: F. Barbedienne, Paris.
French founder's Youth is interpreted as older than German version.

3413. UNCHAINED

Ludwig Kowalczewski   Wk: c1890-1910
Germany.   c1900.   Pt: Brown-black.
Ht: 20½″

3412. ENCHAINED   Unsigned work
Fr. or Ger.   c1900.   Pt: Brown.   Ht: 11″

3411. LA FORCE   by J. Picciole   Wk: c1900-1920
France.   c1900.   Pt: Brown.   Ht: 24½″   Seal #41

3414. HURLING THE ROCK
Unsigned work
Germany.   c1910.   Pt: Black.
Seal #82   Ht: 13½″
Fdr: Martin U. Piltzing, Berlin.

3416. THE ENEMY BELOW   by Schmidt-Hofer   Wk: c1900-1925
Germany.   c1920.   Pt: Black-gray.   Ht: 23½″

3417. DISCOBOLUS
    After Myron
Ger. c1900. Black. 12″
Fdr: Gladenbeck, Berlin.
Ref: Vol. III, Pg. 395

3418. DISCUS THROWER
    H. Keck   Wk: c1900-1922
Ger. c1900. Brown. 9½″

3419. PREPARING TO THROW
    Classical—Vatican
Ger. c1900. Dark brown. 11″

3420. DISCUS THROWER
    Rudolf Marcuse   b1878-
Ger. c1910. Dark brown. 13½″

3421. PUTTING THE SHOT
    Fritz Heinemann   b1864-
Ger. c1900. Black. Ht: 15″
Fdr: Gladenbeck, Berlin.

3422. BALL BALANCING
    By A. Loebe
Ger. c1920. Black. 8½″

3423. BALL BALANCING
    Schmidt-Hofer
Ger. 1912. Ylo-brn. 11″

3424. BALANCED   W/Seal
    By V. Bugler
Ger. 1908. Black. 10″

896

3425. BALL BALANCING   by F. Timpe
Belg.   c1910.   Dark green.   Ht: 7½″

3426. BALL BALANCING
        By E. Hamburger   Wk: c1890-1914
    Germany.   c1900.   Brown.   Ht: 9½″

3427. BALANCED   by E. Hamburger
    Ger.   Dt: 1907.   Black.   Ht: 15½″

897

3428

3429

3430

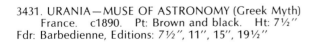

3431

3432

3432. INDUSTRY AND NAVIGATION—Trophy   Unsigned
   Germany.   Dated: 1930.   Pt: Brown.   Ht: 8″ X 16″

3428. L'ETUDE—Research   by Henri Levasseur   b1853-
     France.   c1895.   Pt: Brown.   Ht: 9″, 12″, 17″, 22″
Fdr: Société des Bronzes de Paris.   Seal #8.

3429. DUKE GUILIANO DE MEDICI   by Michael Angelo
     France.   c1925.   Pt: Brown.   Ht: 11″   Vol. III, Page 649.
Guiliano (Julien) was cast in seven reduction sizes
by Barbedienne: Brother Laurent (Thinker) in nine sizes.

3430. ARES, GOD OF WAR   by B. Ludovisi   (1713-1749)
     Italy.   c1900.   Pt: Green-black.   Ht: 9½″

3431. URANIA—MUSE OF ASTRONOMY (Greek Myth)
     France.   c1890.   Pt: Brown and black.   Ht: 7½″
Fdr: Barbedienne, Editions: 7½″, 11″, 15″, 19½″

898

3433. PUGILISTS   Unsigned
   America.   c1920.   Pt: Brown.   Ht: c8″

3434. PUGILISTS   by Henrich Hoffmann
   Germany.   Dated: 1924.   Pt: Ylo-brown.   Ht: 12″

· 3435. PRIZE FIGHTERS   by Borane
   France.   c1925.   Pt: Black.   Ht: 12½″   Seal #62
Fdr: A.G., Paris.

3436. THE BOXER   by Antonio Canova   (1757-1822)
   Italy.   c1880.   Pt: Black.   Ht: c24″
Museum reproductions done in various sizes.

3438. BOXER   by P. Leibküchler   Wk: c1918-1938
Germany.   Dated: 1928.   Pt: Brown-black.   Ht: 26″

3439. BOXER   by Otto Placzek   b1884-
Germany.   c1918.   Pt: Dark brown.   Ht: 11½″

3440. BOXER   by Ledermann   Wk: c1905-1925
      Germany.   c1910.   Pt: Dark brown.   Ht: 11″
Fdr: Robert Sachs, Bronze Warenfabrik, Berlin.

3441.   BOXER by Friedrich Schenkel   b1887-
        Germany.   c1925.   Pt: Gray-black.   Ht: 22½″
Fdr: Franz Grönig, Berlin.

3443. BORGHESE GLADIATOR
By Agasias   c100 B.C.
Germany.   c1900.   Pt: Black.   Ht: 21''

3444. BUST OF GLADIATOR
By Constant-Roux   (1865-1929)
France.   c1920.   Pt: Brown.   Ht: 9½''
Fdr: Susse Frères, Paris.

3446. WOUNDED GLADIATOR
By Luca Madrassi   Wk: c1869-1914
France.   c1890.   Pt: Brown.   Ht: 7½''

902

3445. FIGHTING GLADIATOR
    By Constant-Roux (1865-1929)
France. c1920. Pt: Dark green. 25″
Fdr: Susse, Lost wax. Seal #72

3447. APOLLO BELVEDERE
    Att: Leochares—Greek c400 B.C.
Italy. c1890. Pt: Ylo-brown. Ht: 40″
Fdr: B. Boschetti, Roma.

3448. PERSEUS—Vatican Marble
    By Antonio Canova (1757-1822)
Italy. c1910. Pt: Brown. Ht: 24″
Sculpture depicts Perseus, son of Zeus, with
head of Gorgon sister, Medusa, which he gave
to Athene for her shield.

3449. THE SCULPTOR
    By Huzel Wk: c1850-1890
France. c1875. Pt: Gold-doré. Ht: 14½″

3451. DAVID AVANT LE COMBAT
    By Antonin Mercié   (1845-1916)
France. c1895. Pt: Brown. Ht: 19″, *31½″,* Seal #6
Fdr: F. Barbedienne, Paris. Displayed at Salon
of 1876 and Exposition Universelle de 1878. Never
as popular as David Vainqueur, Vol. I, #679.

3453. DAVID BEFORE THE BATTLE
    By Prof. Victor Heinrich Seifert   b1870-
Germany. c1905.   Pt: Black-gray.   Ht: 28″
French exhibited sculptures nude but founders
modestly covered genitals—Germans didn't.

904

3454. MALE RUNNER
    By Franz Seifert   b1866-
Germany.   Dated: 1922.   Pt: Black.   Ht: 20″

3455. FEMALE RUNNER
    By P. Leibküchler   Wk: c1918-1938
Germany.   Dated: 1929.   Pt: Light brown.   Ht: 12½″

3456. NENIKHKAMEN
    By Carl Max Kruse   b1854-
Germany.   c1899.   Pt: Brown.   Ht: 13″ etc.
Fdr: O. Gladenbeck, Berlin. This work is in the
Berlin Museum titled: Messenger of the Marathon.

3457. LADY HURDLER
    By Marguerite Blanchon   b1872-
France.   1902.   Pt: Ylo-brown.   Ht: 12″

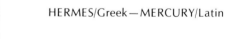

3462

3463. HERMES RESTING
    Italy. c1920. Dark green. 11″
Fdr: Fonderia Sommer, Napoli Museum.
From antique Greek bronze.

HERMES/Greek—MERCURY/Latin

3458. MERCURY SEATED
    A. Thorwaldsen (1768-1844)
Denmark. 1820. Brown. 11″

3459. HERMES AU REPOS
    Marius Montagne (1828-1879)
France. Dated: 1867. Brown. 12½″

3460. MERCURY IN FLIGHT
    Andreas Ruff b1885-
Austria. 1915. Black. 19½″

3461. MERCURY WITH CADUCEUS
    Gian de Bologna (1529-1608)
Italy. c1920. Black. 24″ etc.

3462. MERCURY STANDING   Unsigned
    Fr. c1930. Brown. 12″ Fdr: C.A.B.

906

3466. BUSTE WALKYRIE — Valkyrie
Emmanuel Villanis   Wk: c1880-1920
France. c1910. Brown, green.   Seal #8
Soc. of Bronzes, *10″, 17½″, 25″, 31½″*
In Norse mythology, the maidens of Odin
conducted slain battle heroes to the
halls of Valhalla.

3465. VINCERE AUT MORIOR
By Emile Picault   b1839-
France. c1980. Green-brown.   Ht: 35″

3467. RACING TROPHY   by E. Saalmann   Wk: c1918-1932
      Germany.   Dated: 1922.   Pt: Brown.   Ht: 7½″
Fdr: M.B.V. Echte-Bronce, Köln. (Cologne)

3468. SAILING TROPHY   by P. Marius Jensen   b1883-
      Germany.   c1915.   Pt: Green-brown.   Ht: 8½″

3469. FENCER AT REST   Unsigned work   Wh-Met.
      Sweden.   c1935.   Pt: Aluminum.   Ht: 12″

3470. VICTOR'S TROPHY   Unsigned work
      Germany.   c1910.   Pt: Black.   Ht: 15½″

3471. TO THE VICTOR   by L. Graefner
      Germany.   c1910.   Pt: Brown.   Ht: 11½″

3472. TO THE VICTOR   H. Keck   Wk: c1900-1922
      Germany.   c1910.   Pt: Black.   Ht: c11″

3473. THRUST OF KNIGHT   by Rudolf Küchler   b1867-
      Germany.   c1900.   Pt: Brown.   Ht: 13″

3474. DUELIST'S LUNGE   by Rudolf Küchler   b1867-
      Germany.   c1900.   Pt: Gold, brown.   Ht: 14½″

347A. SON OF ERIC   Unsigned work
      France.   c1880.   Pt: Gray-black.   Ht: c11″

3475. KNOWLEDGE-VICTORY
      By Johannes Götz   b1865-
Germany.   1898.   Pt: Brown-green.   Ht: 14½″

3472

3473

3474

347A

3475

909

3478. VIRTUTES CIVICAE—Ense et Labore
By Emile L. Picault   Wk: c1860-1915
France.   c1895.   Blue, green, brown.   Ht: 26″
Edited in smaller and larger sizes.

3477. PRO MERITO—Latin
By Emile Louis Picault   b1839-
France.   c1880.   Pt: Brown.   Ht: 20″
Edited in smaller and larger sizes.

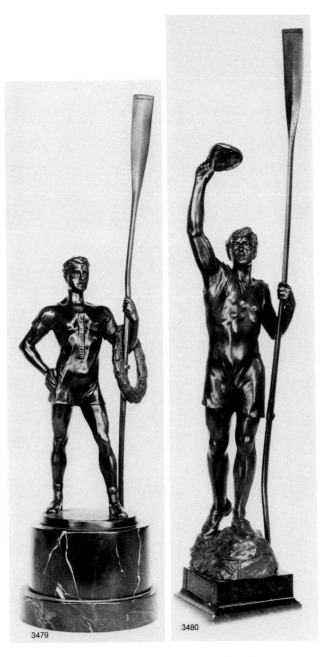

3479. ROWING TROPHY   Unsigned work
   France.   c1920.   Pt: Brown.   Ht: 13½″
Founder's monogram: Diamond M.

3480. ROWING TROPHY
   By Müller-Krefeld   b1863-
Germany.   c1900.   Pt: Light brown.   Ht: 23½″

3481. VICTOR   by E. Beck   Wk: c1890-1925
   Germany.   c1920.   Pt: Green.   Ht: 19½″

3482. VICTORY BRANCH
   By Schmidt-Felling   Wk: c1895-1930
Germany.   c1920.   Pt: Brown.   Ht: 19″

3483. PEACE—HONOR
   By Sidney March   Wk: c1890-1910
England.   Dated: 1895.   Pt: Black.   Ht: 28″

3484

3487

3485

3486

ST. JOAN OF ARC

Heroine and a patron saint of France (1412-1431) was inspired by supernatural voices. She led the French against the English to free Orleans and aided in the coronation of Charles VII at Reims. At age nineteen she was taken prisoner by the English, tried as a witch by an ecclesiastical tribunal, and burned public-ly at the stake.

Years later she was declared innocent of all charges by a higher ecclesiastical authority and finally cannonized in 1920. Known also as the Maid of Orleans. Because of her great strength, per-sistent rumor says she was a boy.

3484. JEANNE D'ARC
   By Ernest Casini   Wk: c1885-1915
France.   c1900.   Pt: Dark brown.   Ht: 29½''

3485. JEANNE D'ARC
   By Antoine Bofill   Wk: c1895-1925
France.   c1910.   Pt: Silver gold/ivory.   Ht: 13½''
Fdr: H.V. Bronze D'Art, Paris.

3486. JEANNE D'ARC   Unsigned work   White-metal
   France.   c1920.   Pt: Green-brown.   Ht: 10'' head.

3487. JEANNE D'ARC PRISONNIÈRE
   By Louis-Ernest Barrias (1841-1905)
Fr. Salon: 1892.   Silver, gold/ivory.
Fdr: Susse Frères, Paris. Ht: *15''*, 20'', etc.
Ref: Vol. III, #2513.   Seal #12

3488. LES AMANTS
By Ernest Rancoulet   Wk: c1870-1915
France.   c1885.   Pt: Gold-brown.   Ht: 31"   Wh-met.

3489. PAIX AND PROGRESS
By Emile Bruchon   Wk: c1880-1910
France.   c1890.   Pt: Choc-brown.   Ht: 31"   Wh-met.

3490

3491

3490. JEANNE D'ARC   by Adrien-Etienne Gaudez   (1845-1902)
France.   Dated: 1888.   Pt: Choc-brown.   Ht: 30½''

3491. JEANNE D'ARC
   By Georges Omerth   Wk: c1895-1925
France.   c1902.   Pt: Gold-brown.   Ht: 25''

3492. JEANNE D'ARC
   By Ruffony   Wk: c1900-1925
France.   c1915.   Pt: Brown.   Ht: 7½''
Fdr: Montoy Edtrs., Paris.

3492

3493

3495

3493. JEANNE D'ARC
By Etienne-Henri Dumaige (1830-1888)
France. c1875. Pt: Brown. Ht: 18½″ Seal #18

3495. JEANNE D'ARC
By Edouard Drouot (1859-1945)
France. c1900. Pt: Ylo-brown. Ht: c30″

3498. FISHERMAN'S PRIZE   by Ludwig Vordermayer   b1868-
Germany.   c1910.   Pt: Dark brown.   Ht: 12"
Founder: Finzel, Berlin.

3497. REWARD OF THE HUNT   by Pierre Andrée
Fr. or Ger.   c1910.   Pt: Brown-green.   Ht: 23½"

3496. HUNTER'S PRIZE   by Schmidt-Felling   Wk: c1895-1930
Germany.   c1910.   Pt: Brown-black.   Ht: 34½"

3499. ARCHER'S TROPHY Victor Oskar Tilgner (1844-1896)
    Germany. c1910. Pt: Green-brown. Ht: 16½"
Fdr: V.R. Bransch Bildbuss, Hambourg.

3500. VICTOR OF THE HUNT by Schmidt-Hofer Wk: 1900-1925
    Germany. c1910. Pt: Brown. Ht: 12¼"

3501. VICTORIOUS ARCHER by Josef Uphues (1850-1911)
    Germany. c1890. Pt: Dark brown. Ht: 14½", 19"
Fdr: Gladenbeck-Friedrich & Shoger, Berlin.

917

3505. ROMAN BOWMAN   by Schmidt-Hofer   Wk: c1900-1925.
Germany.   c1900.   Pt: Dark brown.   Ht: *18½″, 12½″*

3503. ACTÉON   by Emile-Henri LaPorte   (1841-1919)
France. Salon: 1879.   Pt: Brown.   Ht: 32″
Fdr: Siot-Decauville, Paris. Editions: 21½″, 14″, 6½″

Actaeon was a great hunter who came across Artemis
disrobed. She changed him into a stag to be torn
apart by his own hounds.

918

3506

3507

3508

350 A

3506. QUARRY SEEKER   by Emil Manz   b1880-
     Germany.   Dated: 1913.   Pt: Dark brown.   Ht: 25″

3507. BOWMAN—After the Shot
     By Rudolf Küchler Fec. (Fecit—I did it)
Germany.   c1910.   Pt: Green-black.   Ht: 20″

3508. STRINGING THE BOW   BY Otto Riese   (1851-1910)
     Germany.   c1900.   Pt: Dark brown.   Ht: 10″
Fdr: K.B. Echte Bronze, Munich.

350A. MASTER AND STUDENT   Unsigned work
     France.   c1850.   Pt: Brown black.   Ht: 16″
In the style of Francois Rude   (1784-1855)

3509

3510

3511

3512

3509. YOUNG ARCHER   by R.W. Lange
       Fr. or Ger.   c1920.   Pt: Black.   Ht: 9″

3510. SKYWARD ARROW   Unsigned work
       Germany.   c1910.   Pt: Black.   Ht: 21″

3511. THE ARCHER   by Hans Haffenrichter   b1897-
       Germany.   c1930.   Pt: Gray-brown.   Ht: 22½″
Fdr: Guss. G. Heinze, Berlin.

3512. SHOOTING THE SUN   by August Bischoff
       Germany.   c1910.   Pt: Brown-black.   Ht: 21″

3514. ARCHER   by Schmotz-Metzner
       Germany.   c1920.   Pt: Dark brown.   Ht: 23″

3515. ARCHERY FORM   by J. Wiesing
       Germany.   c1910.   Pt: Gray-brown.   Ht: 15½″

3516. RUNNING ARCHER   by Schmidt-Hofer
       Germany.   c1910.   Pt: Jet black.   Ht: 15″

351A. SUN SHOT   by Schmidt-Felling
   Wk: c1895-1930
   Germany.   c1910.
   Pt: Green-brown.   Ht: 11″

3517. THE ARCHER   by Karl Kowalczewski   b1876-   351B. TRACK TROPHY   by Rudolf Küchler   b1867-
   Germany.   c1910.   Pt: Green-black.   Ht: 11″   Germany.   c1900.   Pt: Black.   Ht: 10″

3518

3519

3520

3520. ARCHERESS   by H. Keck   Wk: c1900-1922
Germany. c1920. Pt: Yellow. Ht: 9″
Fdr: Wiener＝Kanstwerkstättes: Brandel, Berlin.

3519. LADY ARCHER—Artemis
By Ferdinand Lepke/Lepcke (1866-1909)
Germany. c1900.   Pt: Dark brown.   Ht: 20″

3518. DIANE CHASSERESSE   Wh-Met.
By Auguste Guillemin (1848-1909)
France. c1895.   Pt: Yellow.   Ht: 34″   Seal #20

3522. DIANE THE HUNTRESS
   By A.E. Dubucand Fils.   Wk: c1880-1900
France.   c1890.   Pt: Dark brown.   Ht: 36″
   Probably son of Alfred Dubucand.

3524. DIANE VICTORIEUSE
   By Albert-Ernest Carrier-Belleuse   (1824-1887)
France.   Dated: 1889.   Pt: Yellow. Ht: 26″   Base 5″
Exhibited in plaster at salon of 1885, in marble in
1887, and bronze 1888. Has seal of Expo. 1889.

923

3525

3526

3527

3528

3529

3525-6. PORTUGUESE SOLDIERS (15th Cen.)
France. c1880. Pt: Brown. Ht: 11″

3527. PIZARRE (1470-1541) White-Metal
France. c1900. Pt: Gray. Ht: 18½″
Francisco Pizarro, Spanish conqueror of Peru.

3528-9. CONQUISTADORES (14th Century)
France. c1880. Pt: Silver black. 21″ Wh-Met.

3530. HERNANDO CORTEZ (1485-1547) Wh-Met.
France. c1900. Pt: Gray. Ht: 19″
Cortez, Spanish explorer/conqueror of Mexico.

3531-2. 16th CENTURY SOLDIERS Wh-Met.
By Pierre-Louis Détrier (1822-1897)
France. c1880. Pt: Black. Ht: 21½″

3533-4. GREEK SOLDIERS-3rd Century B.C.
By Edouard Drouot (1859-1945)
France. c1900. Pt: Brown. Ht: 17″

3530

3531

3532

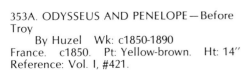

353A

353A. ODYSSEUS AND PENELOPE—Before
Troy
    By Huzel   Wk: c1850-1890
France.   c1850.   Pt: Yellow-brown.   Ht: 14''
Reference: Vol. I, #421.

3533

3534

3536

Le Coup de l'Etrier

926

3538

EMILE-LOUIS PICAULT
Active: c1860-1915

In the field of romantic bronzes, 1800-1930, Picault has recently become one of the most widely known and collected French sculptors. His 1000 plus editions were cast by at least a dozen of the finest Parisian founders.

3536. LE COUP DE L'ETRIER
By Emile-Louis Picault b1839-
France. c1875. Pt: Dark brown. Ht: 25"
Title, *Stirrup-Cup*, is an archaism for the farewell drink given to an inn guest. Picault invites viewer to reflect upon this special guest's romantic visit.

3538. ESCHOLIER, 14th SIECLE
By Emile-Louis Picault b1839-
France. c1855. Pt: Tones of brown.   Ht: 32½"
Fdr: Boyer Frès. à Paris. Six Hts. & w/ivory.
Example is complete/original less bookmark.
"Scholar" comes between Picault's Archer 13th Century and La Basoche—Clerk of Justice 15th Century, cast 30", 25", 18½" by Société/des Bronzes.

3539

3540

3539-40. PHAROAHS OF ANCIENT EGYPT
By Emile-Louis Picault   b1839-
France.   c1890.   Pt: Black.   Ht: 28½″

Marble base is red, white and black 10″. Bronze caryatids,
plaque and pyramid slope add mystical flavor to this pair.
Smaller editions were done on standard type bronze base.

928

3541. GENIUS OF LABOR
  By E.L. Picault   b1839-
France.   c1895.   Pt: Black.   Ht: 30″
First proof cast is left unfinished with
Roman joining-pins visible.

3541

3544

3543

3542. INDECISIVE MOMENT   by W. Jypagne
    Austria.   c1905.   Pt: Brown.   Ht: 12″ X 16½″
Founder's monogram: B. over S.

3543. GOOD TIME TROIKA
    By C. Hans Guradze   b1861-
Germany.   c1915.   Pt: Brown.   Ht: 7″ X 18″
Founder: Offenhausen, Berlin.

3544. FORGOTTEN BASKET
    By Jean Revillon   (1819-1869)
France.   c1860.   Pt: Dark brown.   Ht: 7″

3545. PARTING EMBRACE
    By Ivanovitch Gratcheff   (1860-1893)
Russia.   c1875.   Pt: Brown tones.   Ht: 12½″
Fabricator: C.E. Woerffel, St. Petersburg.

3545

3546

3547

3546. NIKOLAUS JACQUES
   By Vladimirovitch Posen b1849-
Russia. c1978. Pt: Gold-doré. Ht: 20½''

3547. SLEIGH IN WINTER
   By Friedrich Gornik Wk: c1895-1925
Austria. c1910. Pt: Green-brown. Ht: 8'' X 17''
Founder's monogram: A.R.   Seal #58

3548

3549

3551

3550

3548. MANEUVER CIRCUMVENT
    By Ivan. Gratcheff   (1860-1893)
Russia.   c1890.   Pt: Brown.   Ht: 7½''

3549. THIRSTY COSSACK   Wh-Met.
    France.   c1910.   Pt: Brown.   Ht: 7''

3550. THE DRINKING HOLE
    Ievgueni Alex. Lanceray   (1848-1886)
Russia.   c1880.   Pt: Red-brown.   Ht: 23''

3551. COSSACK CAVALRY
    Ievgueni Alex. Lanceray   (1848-1886)
Russia.   Dated: 1880.   Pt: Brown.   Ht: 22''

3552. HUNGRY WOLVES   I.A. Lanceray
    Russia.   Dated: 1873.   Brown.   8'' X 17''
Fabricator: C.F. Woerffel, St. Petersburg.

3552

3553

3554

3555

3553. CHASSEUR AU DEPART
Ievgueni Alex. Lanceray (1848-1886)
Russia. c1875. Brown. Ht: 10½″
Fdr: Chopin, Volhynia (Pol-Rus. border)
Chasseur au Retour completed same year.

3554. ARABE KROUMIR by Lanceray
Russia. Dated: 1881. Brown. Ht: 12½″

3555. SIBERIAN GRISSLY
By Nicolai Liberich (1828-1883)
Russia. Dated: 1868. Black. Ht: 22″

3556. PRISE—CHEVAL SAUVAGE
  By I.A. Lanceray (1848-1886)
Russia.   c1882.   Pt: Brown.   Ht: 14″
Several under-bases available.

3557. LETTER FROM KIEV
  By N.Z. Tavrilov
Russia.   c1915.   Pt: Brown.   8″

934

3558. COSSACK ON HORSE
By V.N. Kremen
Russia. c1900. Pt: Brown. 16''

3560. COSAQUE PORTE-DRAPEAU
By Lanceray (1848-1886)
Russia. c1880. Pt: Gray-black. 25''
Fdr: N. Shtange, St. Petersburg.

3561. THE STORYTELLER
Innocente A. Pandiani (1820-1901)
Italy. c1890. Brown. Ht: 15″ X 27″
Fdr: Proprieta Riservata,
A. Pandiani, Milano.

3562. CUPID AND LION
By Antonio Pandiani
Italy. c1880. Silver, gold. 7″

3563. LION AND LIONESS
By Antonio Pandiani
Italy. c1880. Silver, gold. 4½″ X 11½″

936

3566. BARMAID'S CRAFT
Antonio A. Pandiani   Wk: c1875-1910
Italy.   Dated: 1889.   Pt: Dark brown.   13″ X 17″
Proprieta riservata, A. Pandiani 1889, Milano.

The Pandiani Fonderia in Milan, Italy was active between c1875-1910, casting works of the family members; Adelaine, Agostino, Antonio, Constantino, Giovanni and Innocente.

3568

3570

3572

3573

3568. PILLOWS AND KITTENS
By Carl Kauba (1865-1922)
Austria. c1912. Pt: Green, gold. Ht: 4″ X 9″

3570. WHOOO'S ON TOP Unsigned
Austria. c1910. Pt: Brown, gold. Ht: 2″
Owl-top screws into sand-box where satyr and
lady frolic.

3572. FANNING THE DANCER
By Nam Greb—Real name, "Thuss"
Austria. c1910. Polychrome. Ht: c5″ X 8″
Sculptor named Thuss did many small "naughty"
bronzes while working for Franz Bergman Foundry.

3573. SKIRT AWAY—Ashtray
Founder: U. Ulrich, Vienna.
Austria. c1910. Green, ivory. Ht: 5½″
Hinged skirt lifts manually. Smoking woman has
ivory midsection.

938

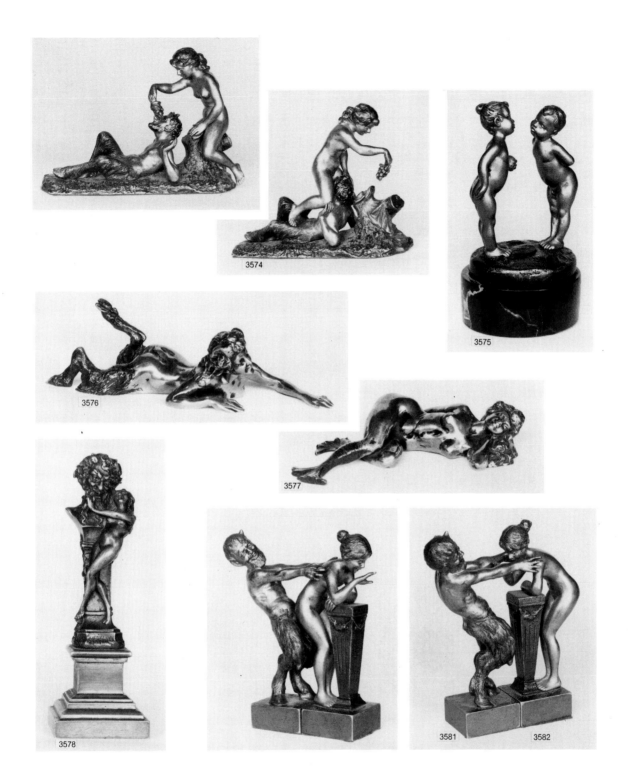

3574. GRATUITOUS GRAPES   Unsigned work
    Austria.   c1910.   Pt: Green, gold.   Ht: 3½"
There is yet a third position to this tricky little two
piece sculpture.

3575. PICK UP KISSERS
    By Nam Greb "Thuss"
Austria.   c1910.   Brown, gold. 3"
Her feet are hinged and springed. When small figures
are picked up by hindsides, they kiss.

3576-7. SATYRIASIS AND MERMAIDEN
    By Joe Descomps   (1869-1950)
France.   c1910.   Yellow-gold.   Length: 9"

3578. AMOROUS AND THE ORACLE   Unsigned
    France.   c1910.   Brown.   Ht: 6"

3581-2. SNEAKER AND SPEAKER   Unsigned
    Austria.   c1900.   Pt: Brown, Ylo.   Ht: 4½"

3584

3587

3586

3590

3588

3592

3589

3584. ON GREAT BOOKS Fdr: F. Bergman
Austria. c1900. Polychrome. Ht: c4″   Seal #77

3586. THE SHEIK'S MEOW Fdr: F. Bergman
Austria. c1900. Polychrome. Ht: 5″   Seal #77

3587. CARPET NAPPER   Unsigned work
Austria. c1910. Painted.   Ht: 4″ X 5″

3588. ENDANGERED SPECIES
By A. Gory Wk: c1895-1925
Austria or France. c1910. Yellow. Ht: 2½″

3589. POSITION IN LIFE   Unsigned work
Austria. c1910. Pt: Yellow-brown. Ht: 3″

940

3594

3596

3598

3600

3590. JUST "FUR" YOU TOO   Unsigned
    Austria.   c1920.   Painted/ivory.   Ht: 7½"
Ref: Vol. II, #1023

3592. BOTTOMS UP BATHER   Unsigned
    Germany. c1920.   Pt: Yellow.   Ht: 2"   Wh-met.

3594. PRINCESS AIDA   Unsigned work
    Germany.   c1920.   Pt: Green, gold.   Ht: 6½"

3596. YUMMY MUMMY   Fdr: Franz Bergman.
    Austria.   c1905.   Polychrome.   Ht: 5½", 8"
    Seal #77

3598. TOPS DOWN BATHER   Unsigned
    Germany.   c1920.   Pt: Yellow.   Ht: 3"   Wh-met.
Mold numbers and mark: J.B.-2039.

3600. SEATED MUMMY   Fdr: Franz Bergman
    Austria.   c1905.   Polychrome.   Ht: 5", 7"
    Seal #77

3601

3602

3603

3604

3601. TWILLING TANZEN   Unsigned work
    Austria. c1910. Polychrome. Ht: c7''

3602. BIG WINDY DAY   by Nam Greb
    Austria. c1910. Polychrome. 13½''   Seal #77
Ref: Vol. I #227; Vol. II #1012-3. All are different—
note feet, hemline, earrings. etc.

3603. HAREM DANCER
    By Nam Greb   Wk: c1895-1920
Austria. c1910. Polychrome.   Ht: 9''

3604. CONCUBINE AND SHAHIB   by Nam Greb
    Austria. c1900. Polychrome. Ht: 7½''

942

3605. TAMBOURINE DANCER
   By Agathon Leonard   b1841-
France.   c1895.   Pt: Golden.   Ht: 9½''   Seal #12
Leonard is pseudonym   for Van Weydeveldt.

3606. DANSE SERPENTINE
   By Jean Garnier   Wk: c1885-1910
France.   Dated: 1893.   Pt: Gold-doré.   Ht: 16''

3607. MARGUERITE   by A. Leonard   b1841-
   France.   c1895.   Pt: Silver.   Ht: 9½'', 19''
Fdr: Siot-Decauville, Paris.

360A. SUN WORSHIPER   Unsigned work
   France.   c1925.   Gold, brown.   Ht: 11'' X 22''

3608. ALL GROWING THINGS
   By Mary Yates   b1891-
England.   Dated: 1911.   Pt: Brown.   Ht: 12''

943

3609

3610

3611

3612

3613

3614

3615

3616

AUSTRIAN LAMPS

These intricate small bronze night lights of the early 20th century were designed to illuminate the scene below in a darkened room. Tiny sockets hidden in domes, tents, under awnings and mats, etc, held bulbs of less than five watts. Condition of original, hand applied paint is most important to their value.

3609. CHESS GAME   c1910.   Polychrome.   21½"
3610. RUG MERCHANT   c1910.   Polychrome.   22"
3611. MUSICIANS   c1925.   Polychrome.   16"
3612. SMOKING ARAB   c1910.   Polychrome.   18"
    Fdr: Nissel & Sikora, Wien.

3613. HOLDING HANDS   c1900.   Polychrome.   11"
3614. LADY WITH SERVANTS   by Chotka
    Austria.   c1910.   Polychrome.   Ht: 15"

3615. BATH HOUSE   c1905.   Polychrome.   17"
    Dome and blue glass water light up.

3616. TEA MERCHANTS   c1920.   Polychrome.   8½"

3617. FIRST CHASE   Unsigned work
    France.   c1900.   Pt: Ylo-brown.   Ht: 3″

3618. COMING AND GOING   by Nam Greb
    Austria.   c1910.   Pt: Green, brown.   Ht: 5″

3624   3625

3626

3627

3628   3629

3630

3631

3619. FOREST VICE-PATROL   Unsigned
    Germany. c1920. Pt: Gray-black.
Ht: 7″

3620. DONKIING AROUND
    By Giuseppe Renda
Italy. c1920. Pt: Black. Ht: 9½″
Fdr: Fonderie Chirazzi, Napoli.

3621. BATTERING RAM   by Wasseralfingen
    Germany. c1920. Pt: Black. Ht: 7″ Iron

3622. RAM RIDER   by Jan Mateta
    America. Dated: 1926. Bown. Ht: 10″

3623. EUROPA UNDEBUM STIER   by H. Krippel
    Germany. 1923. Pt: Lt. brown. Ht: 5½″

3624-9. ASSORTED PUPS
    By Edith B. Parsons b1878-
America. c1920. Pt: Brown. Ht: 5″ to 8″
Founder: Gorham Co., N.Y.

3630. GIDDYUP GASTROPOD   Unsigned work
    France. c1880. Brown, yellow. Ht: 4½″

3631. DOLPHIN FUN by Fred C. Hibbard b1881
    America. Dated: 1927. Pt: Grn. Ht: 4½″
Fdr: A.C.E. Ehberger Co. Souvenir of May 2, 1927
grand opening of "World's Greatest Hotel"—
the Stevens, in Chicago.

3632. RIDE THE WILD DOLPHIN   Unsigned
    Germany. c1925. Pt: Black. Ht: 13″

3633. EROS AND DOLPHIN—Fountain   Unsigned
    Italy. c1920. Pt: Black. Ht: 14½″
Florence or Milan museum replica.

3632

3633

3636

3636. WATER CARRIER   Unsigned
Austria.   c1910.   Pt: Painted.   Ht: c9''

3635. EGYPTIAN WATER GIRL
By G. Chilmeau
France.   c1908.   Pt: Brown.   Ht: 27''

3634. TO THE STREAM
By Edouard Drouot   (1859-1945)
France.   Dated: 1911.   Pt: Ylo-brown.   Ht: 38''

3637. PORTEUR D'EAU   Wh-Met.
By Marcel Debut   b1865-
France. c1918. Pt: Painted. Ht: 12½"

3638. AGUADOR—Water Carrier
By Louis-Auguste Hiolin   (1846-1912)
France. Salon: 1889. Pt: Brown. Ht: 13"
Hiolin is best known in Paris where his works
decorate many important buildings.

3639. PALACE GUARDIAN
By Francois Gaston Coudray
France. c1890. Pt: Brown, gold. Ht: 15½"   Seal #8
Fdr: Société des Bronzes de Paris.

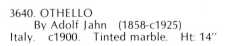

3641. OTHELLO—The Moor of Venice
   By Adolf Jahn   (1858-c1925)
Germany.   c1895.   Pt: Brown.   Ht: 25″
Founder: Oskar Gladenbeck, Berlin.

In Shakespeare's tragedy first performed about 1603, Othello was a highly regarded Moor of Venice who married a senator's daughter, Desdemona. The villain Iago leads him to believe her unfaithful. Othello smothers her to death before learning of her innocence, after which he kills himself.

The story was set to music in operas by Rossini in 1816 and Verdi in 1887.

3640. OTHELLO
   By Adolf Jahn   (1858-c1925)
Italy.   c1900.   Tinted marble.   Ht: 14″

950

3643

3644

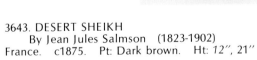

3646

3643. DESERT SHEIKH
By Jean Jules Salmson (1823-1902)
France. c1875. Pt: Dark brown. Ht: *12″, 21″*

3644. AFRICAN BIRD SELLER by Lalouette
France. c1910. Pt: Green-brown. Ht: *16″*

3646. YOUNG ARAB SOLDIER
By Emile Edmond Peynot (1850-1932)
France. Dated: 1883. Pt: Brown, gold. Ht: *26″*
Fdr: E. Tassel Fondeur, Paris.

3649

3650

3649. AFRICAN WARRIOR   by J. Rieder
     Germany.   c1895.   Pt: Black.   Ht: 12½''

3650. ESCLAVE APRÈS LA BASTONNADE
     By Victor van Hove   (1825-1891)
Belgium.   c1870.   Pt: Black.   5½'' X 16''
A Slave Before the Beating is Hove's best
known and remarkably realistic work.

3648. LE BELLUAIRE—The Wild beast Tamer
     By Adrien-Etienne Gaudez   (1845-1902)
France.   c1886.   Brown or green.   Ht: *18'', 24'', 32''*
Exhibited, Hors Concours—not in competition.

952

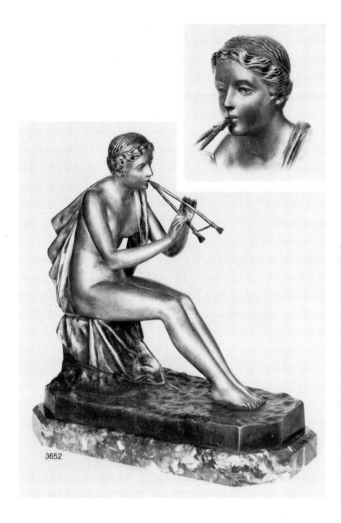

3652. LADY PIPER
   By G. Obiols
France.   c1918.   Pt: Silver.   Ht: 17″   Seal #8
Fdr: Société des Bronzes de Paris.

Also done with longer base and added baby satyr
playing duet on pan pipes with *Lady*.

3654. L'IMPROVISATEUR
   By Félix-Maurice Charpentier   (1858-1924)
France.   Salon: 1887.   Brn., grn.   Ht: 14″, 23½″, 31″

Improvisator was bought for the Museum of
Luxembourg by France after it won second prize at
the Salon of 1887. House of Colin, established 1830,
won casting rights. (Seal #82) The three editions were
carried in their catalog until 1924. Smallest size was
available in Doré for sixty-percent extra charge.

3659. TAMBOURINE BOY
By Franz Iffland   Wk: c1885-1915
France.   Dated: 1887.   Brown.   8″ Base: 2½″

3655. LITTLE SHEPHERD
By Jean-Antoine Aubert   (1822-1883)
France.   c1875.   Pt: Black.   Ht: 9″   Slate: 2″

3656. LITTLE FISHERMAN   by J.A. Aubert
France.   c1875.   Pt: Dark green.   Ht: 8″

3657-8. HUNTER AND FISHERMAN   Unsigned
France.   c1890.   Pt: Gold.   Ht: 9″   Wh-met.

3662

3663

3660. RIDING SLOW   by H. Malavolti
    Italy.   c1925.   Pt: Brown.   Ht: 15″
Fdr: G. Vignali, Firenze., Milano.

3661. PLAYBOYS   by Giorgio Sommer
    Naples, Italy.   c1925.   Pt: Brown.   Ht: 11″

3662-3. FISHERMAN AND HUNTRESS
    By A.E. Carrier de Belleuse   (1824-1887)
France.   c1865.   Pt: Yellow.   Ht: 20″
With hundreds of great works to his credit, this
sculptor has been one of the most grossly
underrated of all time. Stanislas Lami published an
eight page list of his sculptures in 1914.

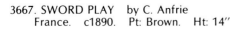

3667. SWORD PLAY   by C. Anfrie
France.   c1890.   Pt: Brown.   Ht: 14"

3664. LE PETIT   C. Anfrie   Wk: c1880-1905
France.   c1890.   Pt: Dark brown.   Ht: 15½"

3665. UN ACCIDENT   by C. Anfrie
France.   c1890.   Pt: Brown.   Ht: 15"

3666. PROUD   M. Lindenberg   Wk: c1895-1910
Germany.   c1900.   Pt: Brown.   Ht: 8¼"

3668. SMALL SMOKER   Unsigned work
Austria.   c1910.   Pt: Brown.   Ht: 6½"

3669. SMOKED MONKEY   by Wegener
Austria.   Dated: 1894.   Brown.   Ht: 9¼"

3670. STREET MUSICIANS   Unsigned work
Austria.   c1900.   Pt: Brown.   Ht: 9"

3671. GOOSE BOY   by Schmidt-Felling
Germany.   c1910.   Brown-green.   Ht: 7½"

3672. A MOUSE   by Carl Kauba   (1865-1922)
Austria.   c1920.   Pt: Black.   Ht: 5"

3673. A FISH IS HOOKED   Illegible
France.   c1910.   Brown.   Ht: 10" head.

956

3669

3670

3671

367A

367B

3672

3673

367A. SEMIFORE MONKEY   by Otty-Furst
Austria.   c1920.   Pt: Yellow.   Ht: 4''   Seal #58

367B. SUPER COCK   by L. Josef Humplik   b1888-
Austria.   c1920.   Pt: Yellow.   Ht: 6''   Seal #58

3674

3675

3676

3677

3678

3679

3680

3674. MOUNTAIN BOY
By Moraile
Aust. c1910. Brown. 2½″

3675. SHORT COAT
By Geo. Omerth
Fr. c1910. Yellow. 4½″

3676. AUSTRIAN BOY
By H. Keck
Aust. c1910. Dk. brn. 4½″

3677. PROTECTION Unsigned
Aust. c1910. Ylo. 2″

3678. FIDĒLITĒ by A. Hannes
Fr. c1920. Brown. 9″
Material: Terra Cotta

3680. CIRCUS OVER
By Enrico Astori b1858-
Italy. 1899. Pt: Dark brown. Ht: 17″
Fdr: Gino Konforti, Florence.

3679. SOUP TIME
By Hans Latt b1859-
Germany. Salon 1889. Pt: Green-brown. Ht: 16″
Fdr: Guss. v. Ch. Linz, Nbg. (Nuremberg)

3681. MATCHLESS LADY by Papke
Austria. c1905. Pt: Yellow. Ht: 4½″

3681

3682

3683

3684

3685

3686

3682. SITTING PRETTY D. H. Chiparus   Wk: c1914-1933
France.   c1920   Pt: Gold, silver.   Ht: 8″

3683. SUZETTE   by Juan Clara   b1875-
France.   c1910.   Pt: Yellow-green.   Ht: c7″

3684-5. GIRL WITH CAT—BOY WITH DOG
By Charles Parks   b1922-
America.   Dated: 1974.   Pt: Brown.   Ht: 8″
Limited edition by the Franklin Mint, U.S.A.

3686. ZEZETTE—Bust   by Juan Clara   b1875-
France.   c1920.   Pt: Gold-gilt.   Ht: c8″   Seal #44

3687

3688

3689

3690

3687. CURIOUS SERPENT
    By P. Tereszczuk   Wk: c1895-1925
Aust.   c1920.   Pt: Brown.   Ht: 6¼"

3688. FLOWER VENDORS   Unsigned
    Italy. c1925.   Gray-brown. 9½"
Founder: F.P., Napoli. (Naples)

3689. SCHOOL GIRLS
    By P. Tereszczuk   Wk: c1895-1925
Aust.   c1910.   Pt: Brown.   Ht: 7"

3690. AFTER THE CHORES
    Constantino Barbella   (1852-1925)
Italy.   c1900.   Dark brown.   Ht: 17"

3691

3692

3694

3691. CHANT DES MOISSONNEUSES
By Joseph D'Asté   Wk: c1905-1935
France.   c1910.   Pt: Yellow.   Ht: 15½″
Natural stone base: 2″

3692. SOME APPLES
By Joseph D'Asté   Wk: c1905-1935
France.   1909.   Pt: Ylo-brown.   Ht: 8″

3694. SUNDAY MORNING
By Joseph D'Asté   Wk: c1905-1935
France.   c1910.   Pt: Brown tones.   Ht: 15″

3696

3698

962

3696. PROUD MOTHER
    By Mathurin Moreau   (1822-1912)
France.   c1875.   Pt: Light brown.   Ht: 31''

3698. SILENT COMMUNICATION
    By Cl. Mirval
France.   c1925.   Pt: Brown.   Ht: 13'' X 16''

3699. WEANING THE NEWBORN   Unsigned
    Germany.   c1900.   Pt: Dark brown.   Ht: 19''
Fdr: Gladenbeck, Berlin.   Seal #82

3700. MISS PIGGYBACK   by E. Zago
    Austria.   c1910.   Pt: Ylo-brown.   Ht: 10¼''
Fdr: Kunst-Erzgiessere, Wien. (Vienna)

3701. L'ADOLESCENCE
    By Louis Albert-Lefeuvre   Wk: c1875-1915
France.   1906.   Pt: Yellow.   Ht: 25''   Seal #83
Fdr: H. Blanchet Fondeur, Paris.

3702

3703

3704

3705

3706

3704. "EVA"   by Marulka
Amer. c1920. Pt: Dark brown. Ht: 4"
Founder: Franta Anyz.

3705. EVE'S FALL   Unsigned work
    America. c1925. Pt: Brown. Ht: 8"

3706.   AGONY AND CONSOLATION
    By Gyula Sztanko b1900-
Hungry. c1930. Pt: Brown tones. Ht: 11"

3707. BABY HIGH   by J. Koca
    Austria. c1925. Pt: Yellow.   Ht: 8½"

3708. BABE IN ARMS
    Robert Ingersoll Aitkin (1878-1949)
Amer. c1930. Pt: Dark brown.   Ht: 3"
Fdr: Roman Bronze Works, N.Y.

3702. DREAMS OF LOVE   by Victor Kahill
    Amer. Dated: 1917. Pt: Brown. Ht: 11"
Fdr: T. F. McGann & Sons,Co.

3703. FLOWERS   by Mario Korbel b1882-1954
    America. c1915. Pt: Brown. Ht: 6"
Fdr: Roman Bronze Works, N.Y.   Base: 1½"

964

3709. MOTHER LOVE   by Emily Spachman
America.   c1920.   Pt: Brown.   Ht: 5"
Fdr: Roman Bronze Works, N.Y.

3710. FACE TO FACE
By Paul-Jean Guéry   b1898-
France.   c1930.   Pt: Green.   Ht: 9" X 18"

3711. BACCHANALIANS   by Pevola
France.   c1925.   Pt: Green.   Ht: 18"
Fdr: Susse, Fonte sur platre.

3712. FIRST BORN   by Brooks
America.   c1935.   Dark brown.   Ht: 23½"

3713. LITTLE REAPER   Unsigned work
France.   c1850.   Pt: Yellow.   Ht: 8″

3714. THE BUTTERFLY   Unsigned work
France.   c1870.   Pt: Dark brown.   Ht: 9″

3715. IMPROVISATOR   Unsigned work
France.   c1890.   Pt: Ylo-brn.   Ht: 6″

3716. FAUNS AT PLAY   Unsigned work
France.   c1870.   Pt: Brown.   Ht: 7″

3717. QUIET TIME   by Moreau
France.   c1890.   Pt: Dark brown.   Ht: 10½″

3718. A CHILL WIND   Unsigned work
France.   c1870.   Pt: Ylo-brown.   Ht: 8½″

3719. WREATH OF REEDS
By Jean-Esprit Marcellin   (1821-1884)
France.   c1870.   Pt: Brown.   Ht: 11″

3720. FAMILY SCENE   Unsigned work
     France.   c1860.   Pt: Dark brown.   Ht: 7½''

3721. SALMACIS—Nymphe
     By Le Baron Bosio   (1768-1845)
France.   c1895.   Pt: Brown.   Ht: 7½'', 9½'', 12½''
Fdr: F. Barbedienne, Paris. Large marble was shown
in salon of 1824 and is now in the Louvre collection.

3722. SITTING WOMAN   Unsigned work
     France.   c1875.   Pt: Brown.   Ht: 9''

3723. THE JEWEL BOX—Clock Top
     By Jean Jacques Pradier   (1792-1852)
France.   c1850.   Pt: Brown.   Ht: c10''
Fdr: Deniere a Paris, 1860.

3724. THE GARLAND   by Marcel Bouraine
     France.   c1920.   Pt: Green.   8½''   Seal #62

3726. NYMPHE DE DIANE
    Lucie Signoret-Ledieu   (1858-1904)
Fr.   Dated: 1891.   Pt: Brn. tones. Ht: 26''
This is one of the most beautiful, perfectly
cast and patined bronzes we have photo-
graphed. The edition so rarely comes up
for sale that it is virtually unknown to
auctioneers and dealers of sculpture.

3727

3728

3729

3730

3731

3727. HE LOVES ME YES—Loves Me No
    Unsigned work
France. c1800. Pt: Brown. Ht: 13½″

3728. THE LOVE LETTER
    By Jean-Louis Gregoire (1840-1890)
France. c1880. Pt: Brown. Ht: 14″

3729. EGYPTIAN LADY   Unsigned work
    France. c1880. Pt: Brown. Ht: 13″

3730. LADY WITH VASE
    By Eutrope Bouret (1833-1906)
France. c1880. Pt: Dk. brown. Ht: 13½″

3731. THE BIRD FOUNTAIN
    By Andreas Ruff b1885-
Austria. c1910. Pt: Brown tones. Ht: 13¼″

3733

3732

3734

3735

TERRA COTTA #3732-3739

3732. BETWEEN HER FINGERS
    By Albert Patrisse   b1892-
France. c1925. Pt: Tan. Ht: 18″
Fdr: Susse Frères Edtrs., Paris.

3733. ORPHEE   by Camille Lefèvre   b1853-
    France. c1890. Pt: Tan-red. Ht: 10¼″

3734. LA VESSE—Danger!
    By Paul Charles Auban   (1869-1945)
France. c1910. Pt: Pink. Ht: 17½″ Base: 3″

3735. WREATH OF FLOWERS
    By A.E. Carrier de Belleuse   (1824-1887)
France. c1870. Pt: Tan. Ht: 20½″

3736. AMPHITRITE—Nereids   by Fernand
   France.   c1890.   Pt: Beige.   Ht: 15″ X 23″

3737. NYMPHE   by R. Roch   Wk: c1925-1945
   France.   c1930.   Pt: Pink.   Ht: 12″

3738. SEATED NUDE   by D.H. Chiparus
   Amer.   c1973.   Pt: Dark brown.   Ht: 16″
Bronze, cast from #3739—perfect recast.

3739. SEATED NUDE   by Chiparus   Wk: c1914-1933
   France.   c1928.   Pt: Pink-tan.   Ht: 16″

3740

3741

3742

3743

3744

BRONZE STORY BOXES

The box makers' craft is shown in eleven different subjects. Scenes are intricate and a magnifying glass will help to discover some of the more minute details.

3740. THE FORGOTTEN BASKET

3741. PICNIC GOSSIP

3742. JUDGEMENT OF PARIS

3743. REAPING THE HARVEST

3744. EROS' NEW VICTIM

3745. A FOREST OUTING

3746. LOVERS' CAMEOS

3747. THE SECRET GARDEN

3748. A STOLEN KISS

374A. REIGNING PEACOCK

3749. AN ASSIST BY CUPID

3745

3746

3747

3748

374A

3749

973

3750-1. MERMEN AND NOING NYMPHE
By Alexandre Clerget   b1856-
France.   c1900.   Pt: Choc-brown.   Ht: 8½″

3752-3. SPRING AND SUMMER VASES
Louis & Francois Moreau
France.   c1900.   Pt: Yellow.   Ht: 21½″

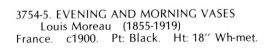

3754-5. EVENING AND MORNING VASES
Louis Moreau   (1855-1919)
France.   c1900.   Pt: Black.   Ht: 18″ Wh-met.

3756-7. EGYPTIAN GARGOYLE VASES
By Charles Louchet   Wk: c1890-1910
France.   c1900.   Pt: Brown.   Ht: 17″

3758

3759

3760

EMMANUEL VILLANIS
Active c1880-1920
Pages 976 to 981
3758. SOLEIL   Paris.   c1900.   Pt: Brown, gold.   Ht: 39″   Seal #22
3759. FARFALLA   Paris.   c1910.   Pt: Brown, green.   Ht: 22″
3760. JAVOTTE   Paris.   c1910.   Pt: Green.   Ht: 3 sizes. Fdr: H.V.
3761. EASTERN WOMAN   Paris.   c1890.   Pt: Grn-brn.   Sizes: 5″-22″
3762. CARMELA   Paris.   c1900.   Pt: Brn-grn.   Ht: 8″   Seal #8
3763. MIRANDA   Paris.   c1900.   Pt: Brown.   Ht: 8″ Wh-met.
3764. DIANE   Paris.   c1900.   Pt: Dark brown.   Ht: 8″ Marble 1″
3765. DIANE   Paris.   c1890.   Pt: Gray.   Ht: 25″ Wh-met.
3766. SALOME   Paris.   c1920.   Pt: Brown.   Ht: c24″

3761

3762

3763

3764

3765

3766

977

3767. SELIKA   by E. Villanis
   Fr.   c1900.   Brn. tones.   Ht: 28″   Seal #8

3768. FILLE DE BOHÉME   by E. Villanis
   Fr. c1915.   Gold-doré.   Ht: 8″

3769. FILLE DE BOHÉME   by E. Villanis
   Fr.   c1915.   Green, tan, brown.   Ht: 18″
Earrings are cast separate. Editions in three
sizes have no seal—founder did not mark Fille.

3770. MÉLODIE—Rêves

By Emmanuel Villanis   Wk: c1880-1920
France.   c1910.   Pt: Brown.   Ht: 20″   Seal #8
Poor quality late casts have been produced in
France with no seal. Smooth skinned original cast,
shown, has seal on back side of base about one
inch up.

3772. MÉLODIE   by Emmanuel Villanis
France.   c1900.   Pt: Green, brown.   Ht: 32″
Fdr: Bentejacs, Cours de Tourny 67, Bordeaux.

3773. MÉLODIE   by Emmanuel Villanis
France.   c1900.   Pt: Ylo-brown.   Ht: 8″
No name on base because bust was taken from
popular full figure, as was #3761.

979

3776. FOUNTAIN TIME   E. Villanis
Fr.   c1920.   Green, gold.   18″ Wh-met.

3775. FOUNTAIN NYMPHE   E. Villanis
France.   c1900.   Pt: Yellow.   23″ Wh-met.

3774. L'ECLIPSE   by Emmanuel Villanis   Wk: c1880-1920
France.   c1890.   Pt: Dark brown.   Ht: 42½″   Seal #8

980

3777 3778 3779 3780 3781 3782 3783 3784

3777. SHACKLED   by E. Villanis
        France. c1890. Pt: Painted. Ht: 5″ Wh-met.
Bust made from full figure, Vol. II, #2244.

3778. LA SIBYLLE   by E. Villanis
        France. c1900. Yellow. Ht: 7½″   Seal #8
Soc. des Bronzes, Editions: 7½″, 14″, 21″, 27½″

3779. CAPTIVE   by E. Villanis   Wh-Met.
        France. c1890. Painted. Ht: 8″
Captive is sister to Almée, Vol. I, #561.

3780. NUDE—Vase   by E. Villanis
        Fr. c1900. Green, gold. Ht: 7¼″ Wh-met.

3781. LOLA   by Villanis Fdr: H.V. Br. D'Art
        Fr. c1910. Grn-brn. Ht: 6½″, 11″, 17″, 24½″

3782. BUST OF LADY   by E. Villanis
        France. c1910. Pt: Dark green. Ht: c18″

3783. BUST OF GIRL   Unsigned/Villanis
        France. Dated: 1921. Pt: Tan. 12½″ Plaster.

3784. CARMEN   by Emmanuel Villanis
        France. c1920. Pt: Brown, green. Ht: 8½″

3785

3786

3787

3788

GEORGES VAN DER STRAETEN

Born in Belgium 1856

Active: c1880-1920

Pages 982-983

3785. MIMI
    By Georges Van Der Straeten   b1856-
France.   c1900.   Pt: Gold-bronze.   Ht: c5″

3786. MURIELLE
    By Georges Van Der Straeten   b1856-
France.   c1890.   Pt: Dark brown.   Ht: 22″
Murielle also cast with large rose in hair.

3787. PAVANE
    By Georges Van Der Straeten
France.   c1890.   Pt: Brown.   Ht: 12½″   Seal #8

3788. JULIETTE
    By Georges Van Der Straeten
France.   c1985.   Pt: Brown.   Ht: 17″   Seal #8

3789. DISH GIRL — Nouveau
    By Georges Van Der Straeten
France.   c1900.   Pt: Brown.   Ht: 18″   Seal #51

3790. NANETTE
    By Georges Van Der Straeten
France.   c1900.   Pt: Brown-black.   8″   Seal #8

3791. A WATTEAU LADY
    By Georges Van Der Straeten
Belgium.   Salon: 1888.   Pt: Brown.   Ht: 20″
One of many ladies borrowed from the paintings of
Francois Watteau (1759-1823).

3792

3793

3794

3795

3796

3797

3798

3792. DIANE   by Heinz Müller   b1872-
Germany.   c1900.   Pt: Brown.   Ht: 9½''

3793. SWEETHEART   by Jean Garnier   Wk: c1885-1910
France.   c1900.   Ylo-brown.   Ht: 5½''   Seal #22

3794. SHY ONE   by Jean Garnier   Wk: c1885-1910
France.   c1900.   Pt: Dark green.   Ht: 5''

3795. BONNET SEAL   by Joaquin Angles
France.   c1898.   Pt: Brown.   Ht: 4''

3796. BUSTE DE MANON
By Eugène Marioton   (1854-1925)
Fr.   c1895.   Pt: Bronze.   Ht: 8'', 14'', 21½''
Founder: E. Colin & Cie., Paris.   Est. 1830
Manon Lescaut, heroine of Puccini's opera (1893).

984

3797. BACCHANTE   by Marie Louise Rollé   b1865-
     France.   c1895.   Pt: Brown.   Ht: 7″   Seal #84

3798. CARMEN   by J.J. Salmson   (1823-1902)
     France.   Dated: 1873.   Pt: Ylo-gold.   Ht: 22″

3799. DREAMS   by Hans Müller   b1873-
     Austria.   1897.   Pt: Grn-brn.   Ht: 5″

3800. JULIA   by Théophile Somme   b1871-
     France.   c1910.   Pt: Bronze/jewels.   6″

3801. EVENING LADY
     By P. Loiseau-Rousseau   (1861-1927)
     France.   c1910.   Pt: Yellow-gold.   Ht: 4½″

3802. BLOSSOM   by Henri Godet   b1863-
     France.   c1898.   Pt: Gold, brown.   Ht: 7½″
Med. D'or. Ref: Blossoms #1551-2, 2258.

3803. LYS   by Julien Caussé   Wk: c1890-1914
     France.   c1900.   Pt: Yellow.   Ht: 22″
Lys was cast in several sizes. Also cast
in white-metal as small as 3″.

985

3804

3805

3804. ERODIADE—Greek
By George-Charles Coudray   Wk: c1883-1903
France.   c1895.   Pt: Dark brown, gold.   Ht: 24″
Fdr: Ch. Gautier, Bronzier, Paris.   Seal #79

3805. LE CAIRE—Lady of Cairo
France.   c1880.   Pt: Red, brown, silver, gold.
Height: 20″. Finest casting, chasing and special
patinization. No signature or marks.

3806. SALAMMBO   by Charles Verlet (1857-1923)
France.   Grn-brn.   c1900.   Ht: 10½″   Seal #22
Signature on bust is backwards—Telrev.

3807. L'VENITTIENNE
By Léon-Nöel Delagrange   (1872-1910)
France.   c1905.   Pt: Gold-doré.   Ht: c18″

3809. GODDESS AT NARA
By Mme. Anie-Mouroux   Wk: c1910-1940
Fr.   c1925.   Green.   Ht: 17″   Susse, Lost-wax.
From original full figure of Seated Goddess in the
Nunnery at Nara, Japan.

3806

3807

3809

ANIEV

3812. MIGNON—See Salammbo #3806
France.   c1900.   Silver.   Ht: 10″ Wh-met.

3813. SYLVIA   by Rigual
France.   c1900.   Pt: Silver.   17½″ Wh-met.

3814. LAUGHING BOY   by Jules Weyns
Belgium.   c1890.   Pt: Brown.   Ht: 24″

3815. SUMMER   by C. Anfrie   Wk: c1880-1915
France.   c1890.   Silver.   Ht: 22″ Wh-met.

3810-11. EMPIRE LADIES   by K. Kowalczewski
France.   c1905.   Pt: Choc-brown.   Ht: 5″

3817

3819

3818

3820

3821

3816. PRETTY BONNET   Unsigned work
France.   c1890.   Brown.   Ht: 13″ Wh-met.

3817-8. COMEDY AND TRAGEDY
    By Eugène Laurent   (1832-1898)
France.   c1885.   Pt: Green.   Ht: 12″

3819. FURY   Unsigned work
    France.   c1900.   Pt: Yellow.   Ht: 4″

3820. SMILING   by Ambrogio Colombo   b1821-
    Italy.   c1880.   Pt: Black.   Ht: 13½″

3821. REPOSE   by Sighieri
    Fr.   c1910.   Pt: Grn-brn.   13″   Seal #2

3822

3823

3824

3825

990

3826

3827

3828

3822. DER SCHWAN NACKEN
  By Hans Müller   b1873-
Austria.   c1900.   Pt: Ylo-brown.   Ht: 8½″

3823. FANTASIA   by Ant. Nelson   Wk: c1880-1910
  Belgium.   c1890.   Pt: Natural bronze.   Ht: 19″
Fdr: H. Luppens, Bruxelles.   Seal #37.

3824. PREMIERES ROSES   by G. Obiols
  France.   c1896.   Pt: Dark brown.   Ht: 22″

3825. FORESTINA   by Mario Digonata
  Italy.   c1900.   Pt: Brown.   Ht: 7½″

3826. FELICIA
  By Georges Van Der Straeten   b1856-
France.   c1900.   Pt: Brown.   Ht: 18½″   Seal #8

After an exciting, successful career in Paris from
about 1880 to the great depression, 1929, Van Der
Straeten retired to Ghent, Belgium.

3827. SERENA   by George Coudray
  France.   c1900.   Pt: Brown.   Ht: 21″

3828. BAKIE   by Geo. Coudray   Wk: c1883-1903
  France.   c1900.   Pt: Green.   Ht: 25″   Seal #79
Fdr: Ch. Gautier, Paris. Ref: Vol. II, #1831

3829

3830

3831

3832

3829. RUE DE PLAISIR
   By Henri Jacobs   Wk: c1910
Belgium.   c1910.   Gold.   Ht: 18½″ Wh-met.

3830. DAISY WON'T TELL
   By Mathurin Moreau   (1822-1912)
France.   c1900.   Pt: Gold-gilt.   Ht: 14″

3831. AMARANTH IN LOVE
   By Luca Madrassi   Wk: c1869-1914
France.   c1890.   Pt: Brown-gold.   Ht: 14″

3832. MYSTERIARCH
   By Paul Berthier   Wk: c1900-1910
France.   c1905.   Pt: Brown, gold.   Ht: 20″
Founder: Louchet & Cie., Paris.

3833. SALOMÉ   Wh-Met.
   By Y. Constant
France.   c1890.   Pt: Black.   Ht: 20″

3834. ATHENE   Fdr: L.U.,33, Paris
   By Cernigliani-Mélilli
France.   c1908.   Pt: Brown.   Ht: 9″

3835. FRAISES AU CHAMPAGNE   Wh-Met.
     By Alfred-Jean Foretay   b1861-
France.   c1900.   Pt: Green, brown.   Ht: 13½″

3836. BACCHANTE   Unsigned work
     France.   c1875.   Pt: Yellow.   Ht: 11½″

3837. THE NIGHTGOWN   by Manin (fecit)
     Germany.   c1920.   Pt: Bronze.   Ht: 11″

3838. LISA   by Secondo
     America.   c1930.   Pt: Green.   Ht: 10½″

3839. ATHENA   Unsigned work
   Italy.   c1910.   Painted marble.   Ht: c26″

3840. NEW BONNET   by Peleschka-Lunard
   Austria.   c1900.   Pt: Doré/ivory.   Ht: 3″

3841. PORTRAIT IN BISQUE   Unsigned
France.   c1885.   Pt: Painted bisque.   Ht: c20″

3842. MARCHIONESS   by D. Alonzo   Wk: c1910-1930
   Fr.   c1920.   Bronze/marble.   Ht: 7″
Other editions in bronze/ivory and all bronze.

3843. CARMEN   by Christoforo-Vicari   b1846-
   Italy.   c1885.   Pt: Painted alabaster.   c20″

3844. NUN   by E. Bernoud
   France.   c1910.   Pt: Doré/ivory.   Ht: 4″

3845. ROSE   by Hippolyte Moreau   Wk: c1889-1917
   France.   c1900.   Pt: White bisque.   Ht: 20″

3846. PRINCESS   by Alexandre Math. Pêche   b1872-
   France.   c1900.   Enamel on pottery.   Ht: 16″

3847. SINCERITY   by A. Gory   Wk: c1895-1925
   France.   c1910.   Doré/marble.   Ht: 22″ w/base.

3848. YOUNG WOMAN   by A. Gory   Wk: c1895-1925
   Fr.   c1910.   Brown/alabaster.   Ht: 18″ w/base.

994

3844

3845

3846

3847

3848

3849

3849. FANEUSE—Buste by Dom. Alonzo   Wk: c1910-1930
France.   c1920.   White marble.   Ht: 20″ w/base.
Gold-doré plaque on gray marble base.

3851

LOUIS CHALON   Active: c1885-1905

Chalon was one of the early and best Art Nouveau
specialists of France. Through his sculptures a
mysterious dream-like quality flows. His art
illustrations are scarce but exhibit the same style.
There, the use of shadows and deep tones add
decadence and depravity to his art efforts.

3851. LA PENSÉE—The Thought
By Louis Chalon   b1866-
France.   c1898.   Pt: Green, gold.   Ht: 22″

996

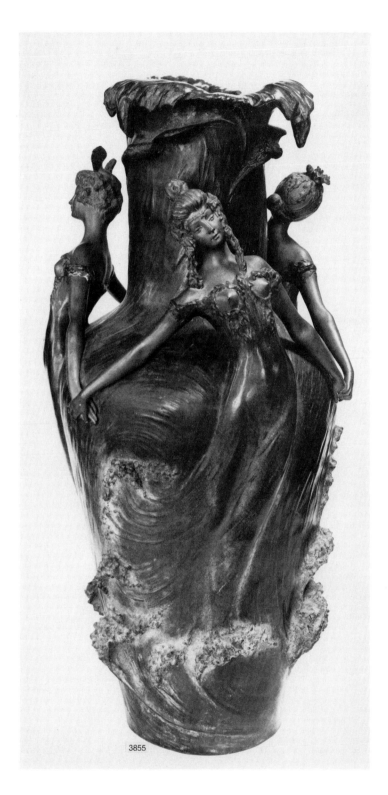

3855. SEA SPRITES—Vase
   By Louis Chalon   b1866-
France.   c1895.   Pt: Brown, green.   Ht: 24½''

3857

3858

3859

998

3860

3861

3862

3863

3857. EROS' LOST ROUND—Vase
   By Jean Jolà
France. c1890. Pt: Gold. Ht: 11½″

3858. BENT FOR SCENT—Vase
   By Léon N. Delagrange b1872-1910
France. c1895. Black, gold. Ht: 10″
Founder: Ch. Louchet, Paris.

3859. STING RAY—Vase Unsigned
   Fr. c1890. Green, brown. Ht: 11½″

3860. WATCHED SLEEP—Pewter Vase
   By Auguste Ledru (1860-1902)
Fr. Dated: 1894. Pt: Black. Ht: 9½″
Fdr: Susse Frères, Paris.

3861. DRAGONFLY—Gourd Vase
   Unsigned work
France. c1890. Bronze-gilt. Ht: 5½″

3862. ROOT HANDLE—Flagon
   Jules Desbois (1851-1935)
France. c1900. Bronze-buff. Ht: 7½″
Fdr: Siot-Decauville, Paris.

3863. ORGANIC FORM—Inkwell
   By Gyula Betlen b1879-
Romania. c1905. Pt: Black. Ht: 6″

3864

3865

3866

3867

3868

3864. LILY VALLEY—Planter
     Charles Korschan   b1872-
Fr.   c1900.   Gold, black.   Ht: 5" X 14½"

3865. CHERUBS—Vase   Unsigned
     Fr.   c1870.   Green-brown.   Ht: 10"

3866. HUG NECK—Pitcher
     Marcel Debut   b1865-
Fr.   c1900.   Pt: Brown.   Ht: 10"
Fdr: E. Colin, Est. 1830, Paris.

3867. LONG HAIR—Letter Opener
     By Albert Reimann   b1874-
Germany.   c1900.   Pt: Brown.   Lg: 7"

3868. FACE TO FACE—Planter
     Gustav Gurschner   b1873-
Aust.   c1895.   Pt: Brn-grn.   Ht: 5"

3869. FROGS BASE—Vase
      By J. Soiram-Petermann
Belgium. c1890. Pt: Grn. Ht: 14½"

3870. CATTAIL—Pitcher
      Cernigliani-Mélilli
Fr. c1895. Grn-brn. Ht: 20" Seal #40

3871. TWIN NUT DISH   Unsigned
      Germany. c1900. Pt: Brown. Ht: 5½"

3872. FOOTED PLANTER   by Lesueue
      Fr. c1900. Pt: Gold. Ht: 5½" X 13½"

3873. OWL'S EYES—Flight lamp
      By Adolf Pohl   b1872-
Austria. c1910. Pt: Brown. Ht: 17½"
Realistic glass eyes emit eerie light.

3874. FLOWER HEAD—Vase by Baubien
      France. c1900. Pt: Gold-doré. Ht: 8"

3875. REFLECTION—Bowl
      By Alexis André   Wk: c1875-1925
France. c1900. Pt: Dark brown. Ht: 9"

3874

3875

3876

3877

3878

3876. TOE DIP—Mini-Planter   Unsigned
    France.   c1900.   Pt: Dark brown.   Ht: 5″

3877. GNOME OF GRIMM
    By Ernest Wise Keyser   b1875-
America.   c1910.   Pt: Ylo-brown.   Ht: 12½″
Fdr: Theodore B. Starr, Inc.

3878. SOUR GRAPES—Urn
    Auguste-Nicolas Cain   (1822-1894)
France.   c1875.   Pt: Dark brown.   Ht: 15½″

3879. INQUISITIVE—Mini-Planter
    By P. Tereszczuk   Wk: c1895-1925
Austria.   c1910.   Pt: Yellow.   Ht: 2½″

3880. MOTHER AND CHILD—Box
    By P. Tereszczuk   Wk: c1895-1925
Austria.   c1910.   Pt: Ylo-brown.   Ht: 2½″

3881. THREE PEEPERS—Planter
    By Charles Korschan   b1872-
Fr.   c1900.   Pt: Gold, brown.   Ht: 5″ X 10½″

3879

3880

3881

3882

3883

3884

3882. PANSY GIRL—Vase
   By Charles Korschan   b1872-
France.   c1900.   Pt: Ylo-bronze.   Ht: 6″
Founder: Louchet, Paris.

3883. COUPE OMBELLIFÈRES
   By Léon Kann   Wk: c1895-1915
France.   c1900.   Pt: Gold-doré.   Ht: 10″
Illus: Siòt Catalog of 1913 at 355fr.

3884. MANPHIBIAN—Jewel Lamp   Unsigned
   Austria.   c1920.   Pt: Brown.   Ht: 18″
Monster's green glass eyes gleem when light is lit.

3885

3886

3887

3888

3892

3889   3890   3891

3886. DELICATE DANCER   by Josselin
     France.   c1910.   Pt: Gold-gilt.   Ht: 10½″

3887. HIGH JUSTITIA   Unsigned
     Austria.   c1900.   Pt: Light-brn.   Ht: 11″

3888. ASTARTE   by Auguste Rubin   (c1855-1909)
     France.   c1900.   Pt: Brn-grn.   Ht: 8½″
Goddess of moon, fertility and love making.

3889. ASTARTE—Bust   Unsigned work
     Austria.   c1900.   Pt: Yellow.   Ht: 2″

3890. JOLI COEUR—Buste   Unsigned
     France.   c1900.   Pt: Brown.   Ht: 1½″

3891. GRETCHEN   Unsigned
     France.   c1900.   Pt: Yellow.   Ht: 1¼″

3885. SYMPHONIA   by Féry
     France.   c1910.   Pt: Gold-doré.   Ht: 10″
Fdr: Ch. Louchet, Paris.

3892. LETTERS LADY   by W. Hering   Wh-Met.
France.   c1900.   Pt: Yellow.   Ht: 13″

3893. SATYR IN LOVE   Unsigned
Austria.   c1910.   Pt: Ylo-brown.   Ht: c4½″

3894. LOST LADIES — Lamp   by Nam Greb
Austria.   c1915.   Ylo-brn.   Ht: 7½″   Seal #58

3895. EVE RESTRAINED — Lamp
By P. Tereszczuk   Wk: c1895-1925
Austria.   c1910.   Pt: Brown.   Ht: 28½″

3896. SATYR'S SONG — Box   by Drah
Aust.   c1910.   Yellow.   Ht: 10″   Seal #85

3897. RECONNAISSANCE   by Hasè
France.   Dated: 1901.   Pt: Green.   Ht: 16″

3898. LECHEROUS DEITY—Inkwell
 By A. Mousson
France. c1890. Pt: Gold-wash. Ht: 2½″ X 13″

3899. LE PARFUM—Lamp and Tray
 By Louis Auguste Moreau (1855-1919)
France. 1906. Pt: Brown. Ht: 18″ Wh-met.

3900. PAPILLON—Night Lamp
 By Julien Caussé Wk: c1890-1914
France. c1910. Pt: Brown. Ht: 24″ Wh-met.
Frosted glass grapes and marble base.

3901. SUNRISE PLATTER   Unsigned
   Aust.   c1900.   Pt: Brown.   Circ: 11″   Seal #58

390A. SUNDOWN—Paperweight
   By Oskar Berchmans
Germany.   c1900.   Pt: Dark brown.   Ht: 3½″ X 11″

3902. FRUIT PLATTER   Mfg: Keyserzinn. Pewter
   Germany.   c1900.   Pt: Silver-gray.   Circ: 10″

3903. FRÜHLING   Unsigned   Wh-Met.
   Germany.   c1885.   Pt: Gray-brown.   Ht: 16″   Marble: 2″

3904. FLORA   Unsigned   Wh-Met.
   France.   c1890.   Pt: Green, brown.   Ht: 23½″

3905. PRINTEMPS NYMPHE
   By Edouard Drouot   (1859-1945)
   France.   c1900.   Pt: Brown tones.   Ht: 24″   Marble: 1½″

3906

3908

3907

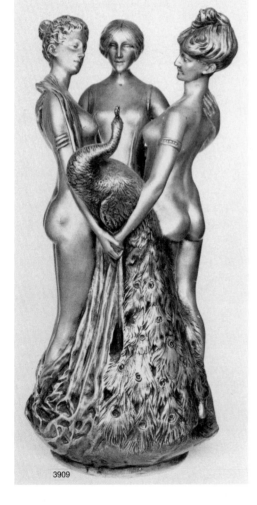

3909

3910

3906. MATERNITY—Bust   by Gruber
    Germany.   c1910.   Pt: Yellow.   Ht: 4½″

3907. RISING NECK LINE—Tray   Unsigned
    Austria.   c1900.   Pt: Green, brown.   Ht: 9½″
In the style of G. Gurschner.   Wh-met.

3908. DANCER'S HEAD—From Genie of the Dance
    By Jean Baptist Carpeaux   (1827-1875)
France.   c1890.   Pt: Dark brown.   Ht: 9″

3909. PROUD PEACOCKS
    By Hans St. Lerche   (1867-1920)
Germany.   c1910.   Pt: Gold-doré.   Ht: 13″

3911

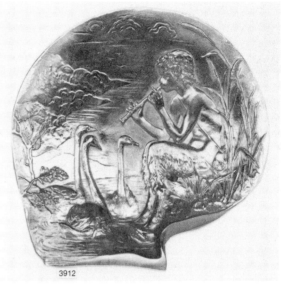

3912

3913

3914

3915

3910-14. DAWN AND DUSK—Plaques   Unsigned
    France.   c1900.   Pewter.   Dim: c12″ X c16″
Note identical border trim is reversed.

3911. HEAD ABOVE—Inkwell   Unsigned
    France.   c1900.   Pt: Dark brown.   Ht: 2½″

3912. PAN'S SWAN SONG   Unsigned
    France.   c1900.   Pt: Silver.   Pallet: c11″

3913. GIFT OF LOVE—Platter
    By Jean Garnier   Wk: c1885-1910
France.   c1890.   Pewter.   Oval: 10″ X 15″

3915. TRUTH—Monument to Flaubert
    Relief Plaque
By Henry-Michel-Antoine Chapu (1833-1893)
France. Salon: 1890. Pt: Gold-gilt. Ht: 6″X3½″
Fdr: Thiébaut Frères, Paris.   Seal #39
Mounted on pale green onyx with beveled bronze
under plate.

3916

3917

3918

3919

3920

392A

1010

3921

3922

3923

3916. WISHING POND   Unsigned work
    America.   c1930.   Silver-gray.   3″ X 7″

3917. THREE WISHES   by Wilhelm Barth
    Germany.   c1910.   Pt: Brown, black.   Ht: 7″
Three Wishes—for one small favor.

3918. REFLECTIONS
    By Antoine Bofill   Wk: c1895-1925
France.   c1910.   Pt: Gold-doré.   Ht: 4½″ X 10″

3919. SHELL WELL-PEN POND
    By Auguste Ledru   (1860-1902)
France.   c1890.   Pt: Natural yellow.   7½″ X 16″

3920. THE SOURCE—Inkwell
    By Maurice Bouval   Wk: c1890-1920
France.   c1900.   Pt: Buffed bronze.   4½″ X 10″
Fdr: F. Goldscheider, Paris.   Seal #38

392A. FLOWING DREAMS
    By Claude Michel Clodion   (1738-1814)
France.   c1900.   Pt: Black.   Ht: 8″ X 16″

3921. EMOTIONS
    By Carl-Hans Bernevitz   b1858-
Ger.   Dated: 1904.   Pt: Brown, gold.   Ht: 20″

3922. SAMANTHA
    By Lucien Alliot   Wk: c1905-1940
France.   c1915.   Pt: Tan.   Ht: 18″

3923. FLOREAL—Night Lamp
    By Charles Korschan   b1872-
France.   c1910.   Pt: Brown, gold.   Ht: 12″

3925. MEDITERRANEA
By Charles Louchet
France. 1903. Pt: Doré, brown. Ht: 15'' X 28''

3926-7. SEA FORMS — Leuchteren
Unsigned work
Germany. c1900. Pt: Dark brown. Ht: 12½''

3925

3926

3927

3929. ÉTOILE FILANTE—The Shooting Star
By Félix-Maurice Charpentier (1858-1924)
France. c1905. Pt: Gold-doré. Ht: 24½"
Founder: E. Colin & Cie., Paris. Est. 1830

Star was illustrated in Colin's catalog until
1924—one size and Doré patina only. Listed
price in francs in that year was 6.360.

BLOSSOMING FEMALE FORMS

3931. NUDE AND VASE
By Charles Louchet
France.   c1900.   Pt: Brown and gold.   Ht: 24½''

3932. FLOREAL—Candlestick
By Jean-Baptiste Germain   (c1845-1910)
France.   c1900.   Pt: Yellow-brown.   Ht: 18¼''

3933. SLEEPING LILY
By G. Flamand/Flammand   Wk: c1890-1925
France. c1900.   Pt: Yellow and brown.   Ht: 21''

3935. WOMAN FLOWER
By Marcel Debut   b1865-
France.   c1895.   Pt: Dark brown.   Ht: 19'', 24''

3937. SWEETEST OF GRAPES
Maxime Real Del Sarte   (1888-1954)
France.   c1928.   Pt: Green tones.   Ht: 20''

3939. ENCHANTED
Joseph Emmanuel Descomps   (1869-1950)
France.   c1920.   Pt: Grn, ylo, red.   Ht: 8'', 15''

3935

3937

3939

3945. NODDING NYMPHE   by Julien Caussé
France.   c1900.   Pt: Grn, brown.   Ht: 12½"

3941. SOUND OF THE SEA   by E. Villanis
  France.   c1895.   Gold, brown.   Ht: 15"

3946. CLOVER LADY   by Theo. Ludwig Tholenaar
  France.   1902.   Pt: Gold-doré.   Ht: 7", 11"
Fdr: Hohwiller, Paris. Lady sits on horseshoe.

3944. PETTICOATS AHOY   by Berndorf Fdry.
  Austria.   c1910.   Pt: Grn-brown.   Ht: 20"
Note string of fish tied to rocks.

3947. MOTHER TIME   Unsigned work
  France.   c1900.   Pt: Brown, gold.   Ht: 10½"

3948. DAY AND NIGHT—Vase
France. c1900. Pt: Brown.
Ht: 8″ Unsigned. Wh-Met.

3949. DEVIL LADY by G. Flammand
France. c1910. Pt: Brown. Ht: 7½″

3951. WOMAN OF SYMMETRY Unsigned
Austria. c1905. Pt: Gold, black. Ht: c12″

3952. LOUISIANA by Louis Moreau (1855-1919)
France. c1895. Pt: Black. Ht: c18″

3953. SALAMMBO by Louis Moreau (1855-1919)
France. c1900. Gold/jewels. Ht: 29″

3954

3957

3958

3955

3956

3958. A TALKING FROG!   by A. Gory
    France.   c1910.   Pt: Doré/ivory.   Ht: 9½″

3959. VEILS   by Nicolai Schmidt (1844-1910)
    Germany.   c1895.   Pt: Gold/ivory.   Ht: 11½″
Fdr: Oskar Gladenbeck, Berlin.

3960. ARTIST'S MODEL   by Peleschka-Long
    Austria.   c1910.   Pt: Brown/ivory.   Ht: 10½″

3961. AMAZONE   by Celestin Calmels   (1822-1906)
    France.   c1895.   Pt: Gold/ivory.   Ht: 19½″

396A. REGINA COELI   France.   c1910.   Ht: c4″

3962. HUNTRESS   by George Morin b1874-
    Germany.   c1905.   Pt: Brown/ivory.   Ht: 6½″

3963. HARMONIA AND DEER   Illegible
    France.   c1915.   Grn, Ylo, brn.   Ht: 8½″

3964. HUNTRESS AND HOUND   Unsigned
    Austria.   c1910.   Pt: Brown.   Ht: c5″

3954. THREE AT SKITTLES   D.H. Chiparus
    Paris.   c1920.   Pt: Gold/ivory.   Ht: 6″

3955. ALL DRESSED UP   by George Omerth
    France.   c1920.   Pt: Gold/ivory.   Ht: 5½″

3956. FROG PRINCE   by Karl Kowalczewski
    Germany.   c1905.   Pt: Brown.   Ht: 11″

3957. WATCH ME!   by Alex Kéléty
    France.   c1930.   Brn, silver/ivory.   8½″

3959

3960

3961

396A

3962

3963

3964

1019

3965. ADELINA   Unsigned work
    Fr. c1900. Brown/ivory. 3½″
Wax seal from desk set.

3966. TOGETHERNESS   Unsigned
    Aust. c1900. Brown/ivory. 4″

3967. SHEPHERDS   by P. Tereszczuk
    Aust. c1910. Brown/ivory. 5″

3968. PIERROT—Inkwell   Tereszczuk
    Aust. c1910. Dk. brown/ivory. 6″

3969. TEETERING   by Anton Schroedter
    Ger. c1910. Pt: Brn/ivory. 6½″

3970. GENEVIEVE   Unsigned
    Aust. c1915. Brown/ivory. 4″

3971. WAITING MISS   P. Tereszczuk
    Aust. 1912. Ylo/ivory. 6″ Seal #58

3972. SITTING PRETTY   Unsigned
    Fr. c1910. Brown/ivory. Ht: 4″

3973. CHURCH BOUND   Unsigned
    Fr. c1910. Brown/ivory. Ht: 5¼″

VICTORIAN HOUSE

3975. S I R A —Black Slave of Fabiola
By Alessandro Rondoni b1841
Roma. Dated: 1873. Black/Carrara marble

All the glitter and dazzle of the 1890
Chicago gold-coast lives again at the
Victorian House Restaurant and Lounge near
Lake Michigan on Chicago's north side.

You enter a casual lounge with nickelodeon,
gold-faced grandfathers clock and hand-
painted and signed crystal collections.

The middle room is decorated with Tiffany
lamps, paintings and European weighted
clocks, etc. Table settings and fare would
please a Czar—on an author's budget!

"Sira", sixty inches tall on a thirty-six
inch marble pedestal is set in a specially
built alcove of crystal panels. This is
the third room—a petit banquet hall. The
last hundred years melts away as you relax
here in the elegant opulence that was the
Victorian Era.

3977. CARMEN
By Charles Jonchery   b1873-
France.   Dated: 1904.   Pt: Gold/ivory.   Ht: 13″
Inscription: Prix de Salon 1904.

3978. CASTAGNETTES
By Sandor Járay (Hungarian)
Germany.   1909.   Pt: Brn-ylo/ivory.   Ht: 12½″

3979. MANDOLIN DANCER   Unsigned
France.   c1910.   Pt: Brown/ivory.   Ht: 17½″

3980. THE CLOICHE HAT
    By Joseph Emmanuel Descomps (1869-1950)
France.   c1910.   Pt: Brown/ivory.   Ht: 17½″

3981. CASTANET DANCER
    By Otto Schmidt-Cassel   b1876-
Germany.   c1910.   Pt: Gold/ivory.   Ht: 10½″

3982. RHYTHM DANCER—Draped
    By F. DeVriez
France.   c1910.   Pt: Doré/ivory.   Ht: 10½″, 14½″

3983. MANDOLIN SOLO
    By P. Tereszczuk   Wk: c1895-1925
Aust.   1906.   Brown/ivory.   Ht: 8¼″   Seal #58

3984

3985

3986

3987

3984. GRAND BOUQUET
    By A. Gory   Wk: c1895-1925
France.   c1910.   Pt: Gold-doré/ivory.   Ht: 8″

3985. SPRING FLOWERS
    By Dominique Alonzo   Wk: c1910-1930
France.   c1910.   Pt: Gold-doré/ivory.   Ht: 8¼″

3986. AU DÉBUT DE L'ÉTÉ
    By Dominique Alonzo   Wk: c1910-1930
France.   c1910.   Pt: Brn-gold/ivory.   Ht: 11½″
Founder: Etling, Paris.

3987. Mlle. MUFFET—Petit
    By A. Gory   Wk: c1895-1925
France.   c1910.   Pt: Gold/ivory.   Ht: 12″

3988

3990

3989

3991

3988. FAN PURSE AND BONNET
   Unsigned work
France. c1900. Doré/ivory. Ht: 9½''   Seal #86
Retailer: Vignes de M.P. Sanches, Buenos Aires.

3989. PRETTY MIGNON
   By Dominique Alonzo   Wk: c1910-1930
France. c1910. Gold-doré/ivory.   Ht: 6''

3990. MEDIEVAL SORCERESS
   Unsigned work Att: A. Gory
France. c1920. Pt: Gold-doré/ivory.   Ht: 11''

3991.REVERENT LADY—Medieval
   By Dominique Alonzo   Wk: c1910-1930
France.   Dated: 1912.   Pt: Doré/ivory.   Ht: 12½''

3992. CYRANO DE BERGERAC
Paul d'Aire   Wk: c1890-1910
Fr.   c1900.   Gold/ivory.   Ht: 10½"

3993. PROPER LADY—Sitting
By L. Sosson   Wk: c1905-1930
Fr.   c1910.   Brown/ivory.   Ht: 9½"

3995. BARDE
Jean-Didier Debut   (1824-1893)
Fr.   c1890.   Yellow/ivory.   14½"
Ref: Vol. I #542—All bronze.

3996. THE BARONESS
Paul Aichele   Wk: c1890-1910
Ger.   c1900.   Brown/ivory.   Ht: 12½"

3997

3998

3999

4000

DEMITRI H. CHIPARUS
Active: c1914–W.W. II
Ref: Vols: II, III

3997. HAREM GIRL   by D.H. Chiparus
    France.   c1930.   Brn, grn/ivory.   Ht: 17″
Ref: Vol. II #1822 — All bronze 9½″ size.

3998. BALANCING ACT   by D.H. Chiparus
    France.   c1920.   Gold/ivory.   Ht: 18″

3999. HAIL   by D.H. Chiparus
    France.   c1935.   Pt: Varies/ivory.   14½″
Same figure with sadder face called Adieu.

4000. FRIEND'S REWARD   by Chiparus
    Fr.   c1925.   Black, brn, ylo/ivory.   Ht: 10″

4001. HAPPY GREETING
By Georges Omerth   Wk: c1895-1925
France.   c1905.   Ylo, brn/ivory.   Ht: 11½''

4002. GYPSY   by Georges Omerth
France.   c1910.   Gold/ivory.   Ht: 7½''

4003. BACCHANTE   by Théophile Somme
France.   c1910.   Doré/ivory.   Ht: 11''

4004. CASTANETS   by Blacz   Fdr: C.S.
Austria.   c1920.   Brown/alabaster.   11''

PHILIPP "Fritz" PREISS

(1882-1943)

4005. VENUS—Offering   by Preiss
Ger.   c1930.   Green, blue/ivory.   Ht: 10''

4006. VENUS—Awakening   by Preiss
Ger.   c1930.   Green, blue/ivory. Ht: 10''

4007. VENUS—Standing   by Preiss
Ger.   c1930.   Light green/ivory.   Ht: 10''

4008. NUDE CARYATIDS—Bowl   by Preiss
Ger.   c1920.   Ivory figures, green onyx
bowl and silver over bronze base.   Ht: 14''

400A. VICTORY
By Jules-Félix Coutan   (1848-1939)
France.   c1900.   Pt: Yellow-bronze.   Ht: c24''

4005

4006

4007

400A

4008

4009

4010

4011

4012

4014

4015

4013

4009. MOONING PIERROT
By Ferdinand Lugerth   Wk: c1885-1915
Austria.   c1910.   Brown/ivory.   Ht: 6½"   Seal #58

4010. PIERRETTE—On Parade
By Alfred Gilbert   (1854-1934)
Fr.   c1910.   Green, doré/ivory.   Ht: 8½", 13", 23"
Gilbert's specialty—Pierrot and Harlequin.

4011. PIERROT AND PIERRETTE
By P. Tereszczuk   Wk: c1895-1925
Austria.   c1920.   Green/ivory.   7½" Onyx base.

4012. BAUHAUS PIERROT
By Roland Paris   b1894-
Germany.   c1930.   Silver, black/ivory.   Ht: 19½"

4013. PIERROT'S GOOSE
By Geo. Loiseau-Bailly   (1858-1913)
France.   c1910.   Pt: Yellow/ivory.   Ht: 6½"

4014. LADY HARLEQUIN—Dancing by Barner
   Austria.   c1920.   Brown, yellow.   Ht: 9¼″

4015. SAD IS PIERROT
   By P. Tereszczuk   Wk: c1895-1925
Austria.   c1910.   Brown/ivory.   3½″   Seal #58

4016. HARLEQUIN LAMP
   By Marcel Bouraine   Wk: c1918-1935
France.   c1925.   Silver, brown/ivory.   Ht: 21¾″
Strong oriental influence seen in lamp and base design.

4017

4018

4019

4020   4021

4017. STORMY
    A.R. Philippe   Wk: c1900-1930
France. c1925. Brown, red. Ht: 21"
Founder: Etling, Paris.

4018. KINKY CLAUDINE
    Bruno Zack   Wk: c1918-1935
Germany. c1925. Green paint. Ht: 16"

4019. EASY RIDER
    Bruno Zack   Wk: c1918-1935
Germany. c1925. Depatined. Ht: 10"

4020-1. HIM AND HER
    Roland Paris   b1894-
Germany. c1925. Doré/ivory. Ht: 13"
Fdr: Ernst Krass, Berlin.

4022. STAR DANCER
    Samuel Lipschytz   Wk: c1918-1935
France. c1930. Doré/ivory. Ht: 19½"

4023. RUSSIAN DANCER
    Joe Descomps (1869-1950)
France. c1925. Green/ivory. Ht: 19"

4024. FIRST FLOWERS
    D.H. Chiparus Wk: c1914-1933
France. c1925. Dark brown. Ht: 19¼″

4025. INTERLUDE by A. Maston
    Fr. c1925. Pt: Silver. Ht: 16″
Inscribed: Medaille d'Honneur

4026. PERFORMING PIERROT   By G. Dumange
France.   c1925.   Pt: Gold paint.   Ht: 9''

4027. PANTALOON THE CLOWN   By A. Puyt
France.   c1920.   Silver.   Ht: 5'' X 10''

4028.   COLUMBINE
By Alfred Richard   (c1844-1884)
France.   c1880.   Pt: Yellow-bronze.   Ht: 24''
Sexy daughter of Pantaloon and
sweetheart of Harlequin, Columbine was
a stock favorite character in early Italian
comedy/pantamime.
Reference: Volume I, page 30.

4029. HARLEQUIN   By Alfred Richard
Fr.   c1880.   Pt: Yellow-bronze.   Ht: 24''

4030. TRIBOULET—Rigoletto
By Gaston Leroux   b1854-
France.   c1895.   Gray.   Ht: 28''   Wh.-met.
Hunchback jester of Verdi's opera, 1851.

4031-2. MÉPHISTOPHÉLÈS AND LUCIFER _____
By Jacques-Louis Gautier   b1831-
France. c1865.   Pt: Brown. Height: 26''
Fdrs: Duplan et Salles Bronziers, Paris.

4033. GOOD HARVEST
    Ernest Rancoulet   Wk: c1870-1915
France.   c1885.   Pt: Brown.   Ht: 22″, *31″*

4034. LE FIL DE LA VIERGE
    Pierre-Emile Hébert   (1828-1893)
France.   c1875.   Pt: Brown.   Ht: 22″
Trans: Early warm days of fall.

4035. ARABE PORTEUSE D'EAU
    Jean Jules Salmson   (1823-1902)
France.   c1880.   Gray-black.   Ht: 12″, *21″*

4036. GOSSAMER DAYS
    Jean Jules Salmson   (1823-1902)
France.   c1875.   Pt: Brown.   Ht: 14″, *20½″*

4037. JOUR DE FETE—Holiday
    By Louis Mathet   (1853-1920)
France.   c1890.   Pt: Brown.   Ht: 21″, *27½″*
Fdr: Maison Colin, Paris. Hors concours.

4038. PÊCHEUSE—À La Ligne
    Mathurin Moreau   (1822-1912)
France.   c1902.   Pt: Dark brown. Ht: 29″

4043. WATER CARRIER   By Andreas Ruff   b1885-
   Austria.   c1915.   Pt: Dark green.   Ht: 6½″

4044. FANEUSE   By Ferdinand Lugerth
   Austria.   c1915.   Pt: Golden.   Ht: 8″   Seal #8

4045. GENIE DES ARTS   Wh.-Metal
   By Marcel Debut   b1865-
France.   Dated: 1898.   Pt: Black.   Ht: 40″

4046. LA PENSÉE   By Emile Picault   b1839-
   France.   c1905.   Pt: Yellow, brown.   Ht: 27″

4047. FLIRTATION
   By Louis Marie Moris   b1818-
France.   c1860.   Pt: Black.   Ht: 14″ X 16″

4039. INNOCENCE   Unsigned Work
   France.   c1910.   Brown/ivory.   Ht: 3″

4040-1. LOUIS XVI VASES—Pair
   By Henri-Honoré Ple   (1853-1922)
France.   c1890.   Pt: Brown, gold.   Ht: 7″

4042. GLANEUSE   Illegible Signature
   France.   c1910.   Pt: Gold/ivory.   Ht: c10″

4048. NAPOLEON BONAPART
    By Antoine-Denis Chaudet   (1763-1810)
France.   c1890.   Pt: Dark brown.   Ht: 12″
Napoleon busts of Chaudet are in major museums.

4049. NAPOLEON   Signed Noël R.   1894
    France.   Dated: 1894.   Pt: Brown.   Ht: 12″

4050. NEAPOLITAN LADY   By Grang Colombo
    France.   c1905.   Pt: Green.   Ht: 6½″   Seal #40

4051. BIANCA CAPELLA—Tiffany's, N.Y.
    By César Ceribella   b1841-Roma
France.   c1880.   Pt: Dark brown.   Ht: 17½″

4052. GIRL WITH A BIBLE
    By Henryk Kossowski Jr.   Wk: c1880-1915
France.   c1900.   Pt: Green-brown.   Ht: 11″

4053. PASTORALE   By C. Anfrie   Wk: c1880-1915
    France.   c1900.   Pt: Yellow-black.   Ht: c21″

4054. DE VIVE FORCE
    By Edouard Drouot   (1859-1945)
France.   c1920.   Green, silver, gold.   Ht: 12½″
Wagon load is red igneous rock.

1037

4055. DISOBEDIENT   By Alex Kéléty
       Fr. c1929. Brown/ivory. 7½″ Fdr: Etling.

4056. SHEPHERDESS   Attributed: C. Kauba
       Austria. c1910. Pt: Brown, green. Ht: 13½″

4057. PUZZLED   By Charles Jonchery b1873-
       France. c1910. Pt: Yellow-brown. Ht: 19½″

4058. LE CAIRE   By Johann Pollak   b1845
       Ger. Munchen: 1887. Pt: Brown. Ht: 19″

4059. PRAYER   By L. Signoret-Ledieu   (1858-1904)
       France. c1890. Pt: Gold-brown. Ht: 17″

4060. PURITY   By Karl Kowalczewski b1876-
       Germany. c1912. Pt: Light brown. Ht: 10½″

4061. IN TRAINING   By Mednat   Wh.-Metal
    France.   c1920.   Pt: Brown.   Ht: 7½″   Seal #20

4062. LE FUTUR AVOCAT
    By Henri Honoré Plé (1853-1922)
France.   c1896.   Pt: Brown.   Ht: 6″, 11″, 22″
Fdr: F. Barbedienne Fondeur, Paris.

4063-4. STREET BOYS   Attributed: C. Kauba
    Austria.   c1900.   Pt: Dark brown.   Ht: 9¼″

4065. A DANDY   By Marcel Damboise   b1903-
    France.   c1930.   Brown/ivory.   Ht: 9″   Seal/Peru

4066. HOODED BOY   Fdr: F. Barbedienne
    France.   c1905.   Pt: Gold-brown.   Ht: 7″

4067. SAILOR BOY   By Emile LaPorte   (1858-1907)
    France.   c1890.   Pt: Dark brown.   Ht: 16½″

4068. OUR DRUM   Jean-Baptiste LeBroc   (1825-1870)
    France.   c1850.   Pt: Black tones.   Ht: 11″

4069. CAPTIVITY   Jean-Louis Grégoire   (1840-1890)
    France.   c1880.   Pt: Choc.-brown.   Ht: 27″

4070. CLOCHES DE NOËL   Edouard Drouot   (1859-1945)
    France.   c1930.   Pt: Dark brown.   Ht: 17″, *30″*

4071. DRINKING   By Karl Kowalczweski   b1876-
    Germany.   c1910.   Pt: Dark brown.   Ht: 10½″

4072. SOCCER   By Bruno Zack   Wk: c1918-1935
    Germany.   c1930.   Pt: Gray-brown.   Ht: 12″

4073. BALANCE   By Goren-Eichhorn
    Germany.   c1920.   Pt: Red-brown.   Ht: 9″

4074. TRACK   By Emile Carlier   (1849-1927)
    France.   c1910.   Pt: Green.   Ht: 18″   Seal #20

4075. THE THINKER   Gerhard Schliepstein   b1886-
    Germany.   c1925.   Pt: Black.   Ht: 8½″

4076. ISLAMIC LADY   By Camille Alaphilippe
    France.   c1910.   Pt: Dark brown.   Ht: 17½″

4077. BIRTH OF APHRODITE — Venus   Unsigned
    France.   c1900.   Pt: Painted.   Ht: 18″

4078. MLLE. AUX YEUX VERTS   By Garband
    France.   c1930.   Pt: Emerald green.   Ht: 16″
Founder: Grandhomme, Paris.

4079. SCARF DANCER   By Fanny Rozet
    France.   c1925.   Pt: Silver, black.   Ht: *12″* 18½″

4080. ENCARNAVAL By Alphonse Nelson b1854-
  France. c1910. Pt: Red-brown. Ht: *10″, 14″*

4081. EGYPTIAN VULTURE
  By Auguste Cain (1822-1894)
France. Exhibited: 1851. Pt: Brown. Ht: c21″

4082. JEAN SANSPEUR
  By Pierre Robinet (1814-1878)
France. c1850. Pt: Dark brown. Ht: 23″

4083. MICHEL-ANGE—Buste By A. Carrier (1824-1887)
  France. c1885. Pt: Choc.-brown. Ht: 20″

4084. LE SÉDUCTEUR Luca Madrassi (1869-1914)
  France. c1900. Pt: Gray-black. Ht: 38″

4085. FESTIVAL BOUND By C.M. Clodion (1738-1814)
  France. c1890. Ht: Dark brown. Ht: c15″

1041

4087

4088

4089

4090

4091

4092

4086. LE NU EGYPTIAN   Unsigned
   France.   c1900.   Pt: Green-brown.   Ht: 37″

4087. YOUTH POTION   Louis Hottot (1834-1905)
   France.   c1880.   Pt: Golden.   Ht: 23″   Wh.-met.

4088. CREVETTEUR   Emile Picault   Wk: c1860-1915
   France.   c1890.   Pt: Dark brown.   Ht: 16″, 21″

4089. FLOWER FAIRY   Jean-Paul Aubé   (1837-1916)
   France.   c1875.   Pt: Brown.   Ht: 17½″, 23″, 30″
Founder: Henri Boileau, Paris.

4090. WANDERER   By Emile Hébert (1828-1893)
   France.   c1870.   Pt: Yellow-gold.   Ht: 25″

4091. ROYAL GUARD—Equestrian
   By Pierre Tourgueneff (1854-1912)
France.   c1900.   Pt: Green-brown.   Ht: 24″
Born in Paris of Russian parents. Specialized
in mounted groups.

4092. ROMAN CHARIOTEER   By Antonio Vannetti
      Italy.   c1900.   Pt: Yellow-gold.   Ht: 15″
Founder: Viguali Firenze, Roma.

4093. ENFANT AU COQ
      By Adriano Cècione   (1836-1886)
Italy, Salon: 1872.   Pt: Brown.   Ht: 12″, 16″
Conserved: Modern Gallery of Art, Florence.

4094-5. ATALANTE AND HIPPOMENES—Greek Myth
      By George Ernest Saulo   b1865-
France.   c1895.   Pt: Gray-brown.   Hts: 28″   W/seal.

4096. NILVIRTUTI INVIUM
      By Henri-Désiré Gauguie   (1858-1927)
France.   c1900.   Pt: Dark green.   Ht: 36″

4097. WAGON DRIVER   A.M. Wulff   Wk: c1880-1900
      Russia.   c1890.   Pt: Dark brown.   Ht: 5″ X 12″

4098. MATERNITY   By E.H. Dumaine/ge   (1830-1888)
      France.   c1875.   Pt: Brown.   Ht: 28″   Seal #17

4099. THE SLEEPING CHILD   Unsigned Work
      France.   c1880.   Pt: Golden.   Ht: 20″

1043

4100-1. EASTERN SERVANTS   F. Preiss   (1882-1943)
Germany.   c1930.   Pt: Poly./ivory.   Ht: 8″

4102. FLOWER SELLER   By Otto Poertzel   b1876-
Germany.   c1925.   Pt: Polychrome.   Ht: 10″

4103. BUBBLE DANCE   By A. Godard
France.   c1930.   Pt: Gold/ivory.   Ht: 13½″, 20″
Georgia Graves posed at Folies-Bergère, Paris 1930.

4104. SEA BELLE   Charlotte Monginot   b1872-
France.   c1920.   Pt: Doré, brown.   Ht: 10½″

4105. SERPENTINA   By Prof. O. Poertzel   b1876-
Germany.   c1925.   Green, yellow enamel.   21″

4106. THE ARCH   Albert Bartholemé   (1848-1928)
France.   c1920.   Pt: Gold/ivory.   Ht: 13½″

4107. HOOP GIRL   By Georges Morin   b1874-
Germany.   c1920.   Pt: Yellow-brown.   Ht: 18″

4108. HUNTRESS   By Georges Morin   b1874-
Germany.   c1910.   Pt: Yellow, black. Ht: 11½″

4109. PRECISION DANCERS   Bruno Zack   Wk: c1918-1935
Germany.   c1925.   Pt: Dark green.   Ht: 11″

4110. ECHO   By Demetre H. Chiparus   Wk: c1914-1933
France.   c1920.   Pt: Silver.   Ht: 11½″

4111. CHICKEN GIRL   By Mednat   White-Metal
France.   c1910.   Pt: Green/bisque.   Ht: 10″

4112. BARTERED BRIDE   P. Tereszczuk   Wk: c1895-1925
Austria.   c1920.   Pt: Brown tones. Ht: 9″

4113. YOUNG LADY   By A. Carrier de Belleuse
France.   c1880.   Pt: Gold/bisque.   Ht: c24″

4115

4116

4117   4118

4119

4115. OUTDOORS   By Joseph D'Aste   Wk: c1905-1935
    France.   c1910.   Pt: Gold doré.   Ht: 10″   Seal #22
Contoured white marble simulates snow.

4116. THE KISS   By Jean Rousseau   b1813-
    France.   c1875.   Pt: Yellow-bronze.   Ht: 26″

4117-8. GIRL AND BOY — Busts   Unsigned
    Austria.   c1910.   Pt: Dark brown.   Ht: c5″

4119. BEATITUDE   By Eugene Rossi
    Italy.   c1920.   Pt: Brown.   Ht: 6½″

4120. UMBRELLA GIRL   Unsigned
    Germany.   c1920.   Pt: Light green.   Ht: 4½″

4120 4121 4122 4123

4124

4125 4126

4127 4128

4129

4130

4131

4121-2-3. CHERUBS   Carl Max Kruse   b1854-
   Germany.   c1900.   Pt: Brown tones.   Ht: c5"

4124. GONE FISHING   Unsigned
   Austria.   c1925.   Pt: Brown.   Ht: 5½"

4125-6. PIERROT AND COLUMBINE
   By Victor Heinrich Seifert   b1870-
Germany.   c1910.   Pt: Brown.   Ht: 5"

4127-8.   BABY PSYCHE AND CUPID
   By Franz Iffland   Wk: c1885-1915
France.   c1898.   Pt: Brown.   Ht: 7"

4129. GOOD SAMARITAN   Illegible Signature
   France.   c1850.   Pt: Brown.   Ht: 7"

4130. LITTLE PIPER   By Franz Iffland
   Germany.   Dated: 1885.   Brown.   Ht: 7"

   4131. L'ENFANT
      Louis Valentin Robert   (1821-1874)
   Fr.   Dated: 1847.   Pt. Brown.   Ht: 9½"
   Fdr: A.D. Delafontaine, Paris.

4132

4132. THE FATES—Restored   By L. Cocheret
   France.   Dated: 1864.   Pt: Gray.   Ht: 8"
One of many versions of headless, armless
ancient Greek marble.   Ref: #1871.

4133

4134

4135

4136

4133. RAPE OF THE SABINE WOMEN
    By Gian da Bologna (1529-1608)
Italy. c1875. Pt: Gray-black. Ht: 13" etc.
The original marble, 1583, at Loggia dei Lanzi has been the subject of many bronze reduction editions. All angles are of equal interest. Style is blend of Mannerist and Baroque.

4134. RAPE OF PROSERPINE — By Pluto of Underworld
    By Francois Girardon (1628-1715)
France. c1890. Pt: Brown-black. Ht: 22" etc.
Large version in garden of Versailles. In Greek myth, Proserpine represents spring and summer which was lost to the world as a result of this abduction. Godly compromise returned her each year for six months.

4135. RAPE OF ORYTHIE — By Boreas
    By Gaspard II Marsy (1624-1681)
France. Dated: 1871. Pt: Dark brown. Ht: 22" etc.
Original marble was placed in garden of Tuileries. Marsy assisted by Anselme Flamen (1647-1717).

4136. HERCULES Unsigned Work
    France. c1850. Pt: Gray-black. Ht: 23" etc.
Shown with apples of Hesperides. Baccio Bandinelli (1493-1560) did a modification of this subject.

4137. REARING STALLION By Gegors M. Brahn
    Germany. Dated: 1904. Pt: Jet-black. Ht: 19½"

4138. L'FORCE By Jean Verschnieder Wk: c1900-1915
    France. c1910. Pt: Sea green. Ht: 26½"

1048

4149. FARNESE HERCULES   By Glycon   c100 B.C.
France.   c1900.   Pt: Black.   Ht: 23"
Ancient Athenian marble at Naples Museum.

4150. BOREAS ABDUCTS ORYTHIE
After: Louis Simon Boizot   (1743-1809)
France.   c1875.   Ylo-brn.   Ht: 19½"   Ref: #2403

4151. BACCHANALIANS   By Drah/Max Hardl II   b1879-
Austria.   Dated: 1920.   Pt: Brown.   Ht: 7½"

4152. TO VALHALLA   By Alfred Barye   Wk: c1860-1890
France.   c1885.   Pt: Red-brown.   Ht: c21"

4154. ENLEVEMENT DE HIPPODAMIE
   By A. Carrier de Belleuse   (1824-1887)
France.   c1880.   Pt: Dark brown.   Ht: *25½″, 37″*
Abduction of Hippodamie by the centaur Phloüs—
an episode from war between centaurs and Lapithes.
Executed not for competition, *Hors concours*. Also
edited in *terre cuite*.

4156

4155. THESEUS SLAYING CENTAUR
    By Antoine-Louis Barye   (1796-1875)
France.   c1880.   Pt: Green tones.   Ht: 29½″.
Founder: F. Barbedienne, Paris.
Half size exhibited in Salon of 1850 was titled,
Lapith Combattant Le Centaure. Centaur, Biènor
and Theseus version, shown here is in Louvre
Museum collection.

4156. FROG RIDES A LADY CENTAUR
    By Franz Bernauer   b1861-
Germany.   c1900.   Pt: Brown.   Ht: 9″, 13″
Born and worked in Munich where he specialized
in garden and fountain statuary.

4158. ROMAN CHARIOTEER
    By Heinz Müller   b1872-
Germany.   c1910.   Pt: Brown.   Ht: 13"

4160. CHARIOT OF MINERVA—Athene
    Emmanuel Frémiet   (1824-1910)
France.   Salon: 1904.   Pt: Doré.   Ht: 22"
Executed for Sevres who displayed their
porcelain version at the Universal
Exposition of 1900. Later acquired by
F. Barbedienne and shown at 1904 Salon in
doré patina.

4162. FALL OF CARTHAGE—Punic War
   Jean-Louis Grégoire   (1840-1890)
France.   c1890.   Pt: Dark brown.   Ht: *18″, 24″*
Founder: Susse Frères, Paris.

4164. JUSTICE AND EQUALITY
   Jean-Louis Grégoire   (1840-1890)
France.   c1885.   Pt: Yellow-brown.   Ht: 37″ etc.

4165. SILENUS AND INFANT DIONYSUS
    By Thyllmani
Italy.   c1935.   Pt: Green and brown.   Ht: 36"

4166. BACCHANTE AND BABY SATYR
    By Claude Michel Clodion   (1738-1814)
France.   c1900.   Pt: Green-brown.   Ht: 19"

4167. BACCHANTE AND SITTING BABY
    By Claude Michel Clodion   (1738-1814)
France.   c1900.   Pt: Green-brown.   Ht: 19½"

4168

4169

4170

4171

4168. GOAT AND INFANTS   By E. de Labroue
    France.   c1860.   Pt: Dark green.   Ht: 16″

4169. TWO AT FOREPLAY   By Clodion   (1738-1814)
    France.   c1910.   Pt: Red-brown.   Ht: 17″

4170. GOAT UP—BOY DOWN   By Boldarin
    France.   c1924.   Pt: Brown, green.   Ht: 8½″
Fdr: Marcel Guillemard—limited, numbered edition.

    4171 WINE FESTIVAL GROUP   After: Clodion
        France.   c1875.   Pt: Brown tones.   Ht: c8″

4175. WOODLAND·WILDLIFE
    By Clodion   (1738-1814)
Fr.   c1890.   Dk brn.   c21″, 33″
Base: Gold doré bronze 4″
Note knurled skin texture.

4176. AFTER THE FESTIVAL—Satiated Bacchante
   By Clodion or Picault
France.   c1880.   Pt: Choc.-brown.   Ht: 7" X 12"

4177. PACKAGE FOR THE SATYR
   By Claude Michel Clodion   —(1738-1814)
France.   1900.   Pt: Brown-green.   Ht: 19"

   4178. SATYRICAL GENERATIONS
      By Claude Michel Clodion   (1738-1814)
   France.   c1875.   Pt: Gray black.   Ht: 19"
Children provide an interesting secondary group
and subordinate plot.

4179

4180

4181

4182

4179. ZINGARA—Danseuse Napolitaine
     Jean-Baptiste Clésinger   (1814-1883)
Fr.   Rome: 1858.   Pt: Brown.   Seal #8
Fdr: F. Barbedienne, Paris. Editions: 22″, *33″*,
41″, 52″.

4180. FRUIT CARRIER—One of Pair
     A. Carrier-Belleuse   (1824-1887)
Fr.   c1875.   Pt: Yellow-brown.   Ht: 33″

4181. LADY FOUNTAIN   By Clodion
     Fr.   c1900.   Pt: Brown.   Ht: 36″
Electro-copper overlay on plaster.

4182. SLEEPING ARIANE—Cleopatra
     Antique Marble in Vatican
Fr.   c1900.   Pt: Brn.   6″, 8½″, 10½″ *12″*, 16″
Founder: F. Barbedienne, Paris.

4183. ATHENE PROMACHOS—Minerva
     Orig. Bronze, Athens Museum   c500 B.C.
Germany   c1930.   Brn.   Ht: 12″, 15″ etc.

4184. MINERVA GIUSTINIANI—Vatican
     Antique Roman Parian Marble
France.   c1910.   Pt: Brown.   Ht: 12½″ etc.

1058

4183

4184

4185

4186

4187

4185. GRECIAN HUNTRESS
　　Mat. Moreau　(1822-1912)
Fr.　c1875.　Choc.-brown.　21″

4186. THETIS—Olympian
　　Emile Hébert　(1829-1893)
Fr.　c1865.　Brown.　Ht: 14½″
Seal #87.
Thetis and Jupiter were the
parents of Achilles.

4187. AMAZON—Huntress
　　Rudolf Kaesbach　b1873-
Ger.　c1910.　Green-brown.　9″
Fdr: B. Krohne, Berlin.

4191

4189

4192

4193

4194

4196

4197

4198

4199

4200

4189. ASKANCE GLANCE   By G. Pillig
       Germany. c1910. Pt: Yellow-brown. Ht: 24″

4191. FOUNTAIN BATHER   Unsigned work
       America. c1920. Pt: Dark brown. Ht: 25″

4192. STANDING NUDE   Unsigned work
       Italy. c1910. Pt: Brown-black. Ht: 30″
Fdr: Fond. G. Vignali, Firenze.

4193. AFTER THE BATH—Nude
       By Hans Schaefer   b1875-
Germany. c1910. Pt: Red-brown. Ht: 12″

4194. FOUNTAIN DANCERS
       By Brenda Putnam   b1890-
America. Dated: 1919. Pt: Brown. Ht: 11½″
Fdr: Roman Bronze Works, New York.

4196. DIANE   By Reinhold Felderhoff   b1865-
       Germany. c1895. Pt: Dark brown. Ht: 24½″
Berlin Museum once held his *Diane*.

4197. QUARRY SEEKER   Unsigned work
       Germany. c1900. Pt: Choc.-brown. Ht: 10″

4198. LADY ARCHER   By P. Leibküchler
       Germany. Dated: 1920. Pt: Brown. Ht: 14″

4199. AFTER THE SHOT   By H. Levasseur   b1853
       France. c1900. Pt: Dark brown. Ht: 13″

4200. INDIAN TABACCO MAID
       By Leon Pilet   (c1840-1916)
France. 1898. Pt: Yellow. Ht: 8½″
Exhibited Universal Exposition, 1898.

1061

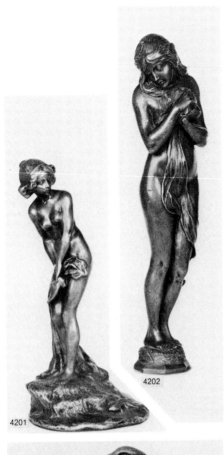

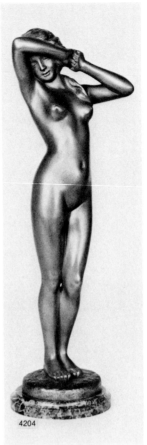

4201

4202

4203

4204

4205

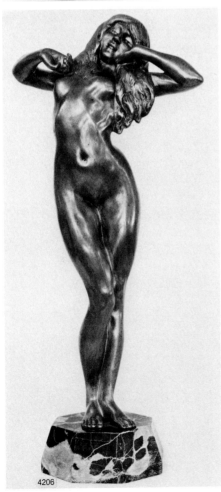

4206

4207

4208

4209

4201. LIZARD AND LADY By P. Tereszczuk
Austria. c1910. Pt: Yellow. 6½″ Seal #58

4202. SHY LADY Unsigned work
France. c1890. Pt: Gray-black. Ht: 6½″

4203. TOP SHY LADY Illegible Signature
Germany. Dated: 1911. Pt: Yellow. Ht: 11″

4210

4211

4212

4213

4214

4216

4215

4204. TRIAL OF PHRYNE   By H. Poirier
    France.   c1915.   Pt: Yellow brown.   Ht: 9½″

4205. COIFFURE   By M. Wise
    Germany.   c1900.   Brown.   12½″
Fdr: Lauchhammer Bildguss, Köln.

4206. MANY CHARMS   By Guiraud-Rivière   b1881-
    France.   c1910.   Pt: Yellow-brown.   Ht: 14½″

4207. WELCOME LADY   By Karl Eichler   b1868-
    Germany.   c1900.   Pt: Brown.   Ht: 8½″, 12″

4208. HARPIST   By Paul Aichele   Wk: c1890-1910
    Germany.   c1900.   Pt: Dark brown.   Ht: 11½″

4209. LADY PIPER   P. Ludwig Kowalczewski
    Germany, c1900.   Pt: Light brown.   Ht: 11″
4210. GOOD LOOKING   By Prof. Tuch   b1882-
    Austria.   c1910.   Pt: Yellow.   Ht: 8½″

4211. LONG HAIR   By Johann Vierthaler   b1869
    Germany.   München: 1903.   Brown-green.   14″

4212. SNAKEN BRESBITTEN   Unsigned Work
    Germany.   c1900.   Pt: Yellow.   Ht: 11½″

4213. GIRL BRAIDING HER PIGTAIL
    By Harry Liebmann   b1876-
Germany.   c1910.   Pt: Black.   Ht: 14½″
Acquired for state of Saxony.

4214. SOMEONE PEEKING   Illegible Signature
    Austria.   c1920.   Pt: Yellow.   Ht: 6¼″

4215. SUPERIOR LADY   By Squelin
    Germany.   c1910.   Pt: Brown.   Ht: 19½″

4217

4218

4220

4219

4221

4216. WATER'S EDGE   By L. Eisenberger
     Germany.   c1910.   Pt: Gold paint.   Ht: 8″

4217. CUP OF WINE   P.L. Kowalczewski
     Germany.   Dated: 1896.   Pt: Brown.   Ht: 13″

4218. WATER CARRIER   George Kolbe   (1877-1947)
     Germany.   c1920.   Pt: Dark green.   Ht: 12½″

4219. THE SOURCE   Horace Daillion   (1854-1937)
     France.   c1900.   Pt: Dark brown.   Ht: 25″

4220. WINE GIRL   Karl Kowalczewski   b1876
     Germany.   c1910.   Pt: Jet-black.   Ht: 19½″

4221. THE BATHER—Antique Marble, Vatican
     Italy.   c1880.   Pt: Green-brown.   Ht: *12″, 16″*

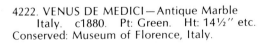

4222. VENUS DE MEDICI—Antique Marble
    Italy. c1880.   Pt: Green.   Ht: 14½″ etc.
Conserved: Museum of Florence, Italy.

4223. VENUS AT BATH—Venus Au Bain
    By Christophe-Gabriel Allegrain   (1710-1795)
France.   Dated 1767.   Cast: c1900.   Black Pt: 21″, 33″
Edited by several founders including Barbedienne.

4225. LA BAIGNEUSE   Etienne Falconet   (1716-1791)
    France.   c1900.   Pt: Brown.   Ht: 16″, 22″, 32″
Marble in Louvre Museum collection, Paris.
Fdr: F. Barbedienne, Paris.   Seal #6

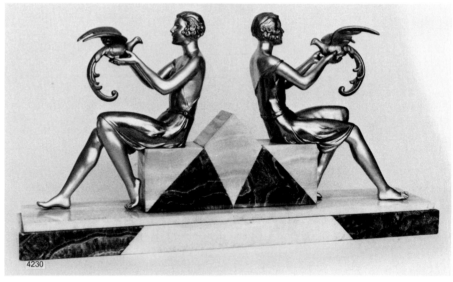

4226. PET PARROT   By Gothilf Jaeger   b1871-
  Germany.   c1910.   Pt: Yellow.   Ht: 17″

4227. FEATHERED FRIEND   Gustav Jaeger   b1880-
  Germany.   c1910.   Pt: Green.   Ht: 10½″

4228. BIRDS OF PARADISE   By C.J.R. Colinet
  Fr. c1925.   Pt: Copper plated over bisque. 18″

4229. SMALL, THE ECHO   By Andreas
  France.   c1910.   Pt: Yellow-brown.   Ht: 11″

4230. L'JUMELLES   By J. Dauvergne   Wh.-Metal
  Fr.   c1925.   Pt: Polychrome.   Ht: 19″ X 11″

4231. DRINKING   By Müller-Crefeld   b1863-
  Germany.   c1900.   Pt: Dark brown.   Ht: 13½″

4232. DRINKING   Unsigned Work
  Germany.   c1910.   Red-brown.   Ht: 10″

4233. OFFERING   By Florence Wentfil
  Germany.   Dated: 1910.   Light brown.   Ht: 14″

4234. OFFERING   By R. Jaeger
  Germany.   c1910.   Pt: Brown.   Ht: 11½″

4235. RÉVEIL   By Philips
  France.   c1910.   Pt: Yellow.   Ht: 15″

4236. WATER CARRIER   By H. Keck   Wk: c1900-1922
Germany.   c1920.   Pt: Yellow paint.   Ht: 11″

4237. AT THE SPRING   Robert Rudolfi   b1884-
Swiss.   c1910.   Pt: Gold, green.   Ht: 10″

1067

4238

4239

4240

4241

4242

4238. FLEEING—The Fox   By M. Guiraud-Rivière   b1881-
France.   c1920.   Pt: Yellow and brown.   Ht: 9″   Seal #12

4239. LE CIEL SUR LA TERRE   G. Kerverseau   Wk: c1887-1893
France.   c1890.   Pt: Golden brown.   Ht: 9″, 12½″, 17″

4240. DAPHNÉ POURSUIVIE PAR APOLLON
By Jules-Alfred-Alexandre Dercheu   (1864-1912)
France.   c1900.   Patina: Yellow-brown.   Ht: 12″

4241. WATER FORMS   After: Alphonse Mucha   (1860-1939)
Czech.   c1905.   Pt: Gold and brown.   Ht: 14″

4242. GOOSE DANCER   By F. Hans Petschke   b1884-
Germany.   Dated: 1933.   Pt: Brown.   Ht: 11½″

4243. SATISFACTION   By Arthur Imanuel Loewenthal   b1879-
Austria.   c1910.   Patina: Black.   Ht: 10″

4244. EXULTATION   By Harriet W. Frishmuth   b1880-
America.   Dated: 1926.   Pt: Brown.   12″   Fdr: Gorham, N.Y.

4246. DREAM GIRL   By Rudolph Kaesbach   b1873-
Germany.   Dated: 1908.   Pt: Green-brown.   Ht: 37″

4247. FISHERMAN'S DAUGHTER   Harriet W. Frishmuth   b1880-
America.   Dated: 1929.   Patina: Sea green.   Ht: 15½″
Founder: Roman Bronze Works, New York.

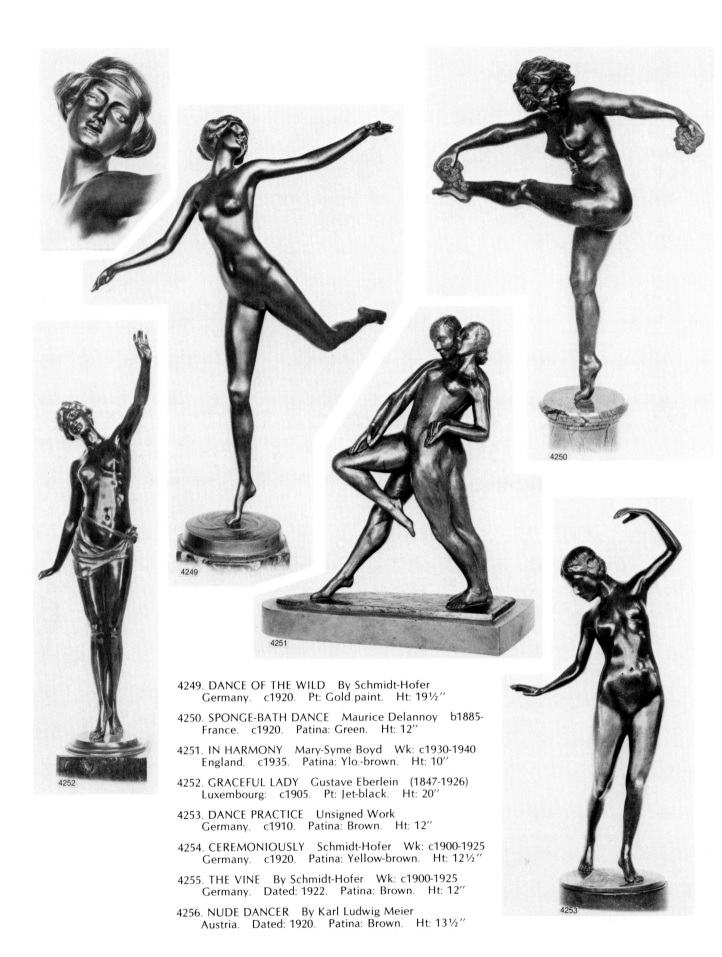

4249. DANCE OF THE WILD   By Schmidt-Hofer
Germany.   c1920.   Pt: Gold paint.   Ht: 19½″

4250. SPONGE-BATH DANCE   Maurice Delannoy   b1885-
France.   c1920.   Patina: Green.   Ht: 12″

4251. IN HARMONY   Mary-Syme Boyd   Wk: c1930-1940
England.   c1935.   Patina: Ylo.-brown.   Ht: 10″

4252. GRACEFUL LADY   Gustave Eberlein   (1847-1926)
Luxembourg: c1905.   Pt: Jet-black.   Ht: 20″

4253. DANCE PRACTICE   Unsigned Work
Germany.   c1910.   Patina: Brown.   Ht: 12″

4254. CEREMONIOUSLY   Schmidt-Hofer   Wk: c1900-1925
Germany.   c1920.   Patina: Yellow-brown.   Ht: 12½″

4255. THE VINE   By Schmidt-Hofer   Wk: c1900-1925
Germany.   Dated: 1922.   Patina: Brown.   Ht: 12″

4256. NUDE DANCER   By Karl Ludwig Meier
Austria.   Dated: 1920.   Patina: Brown.   Ht: 13½″

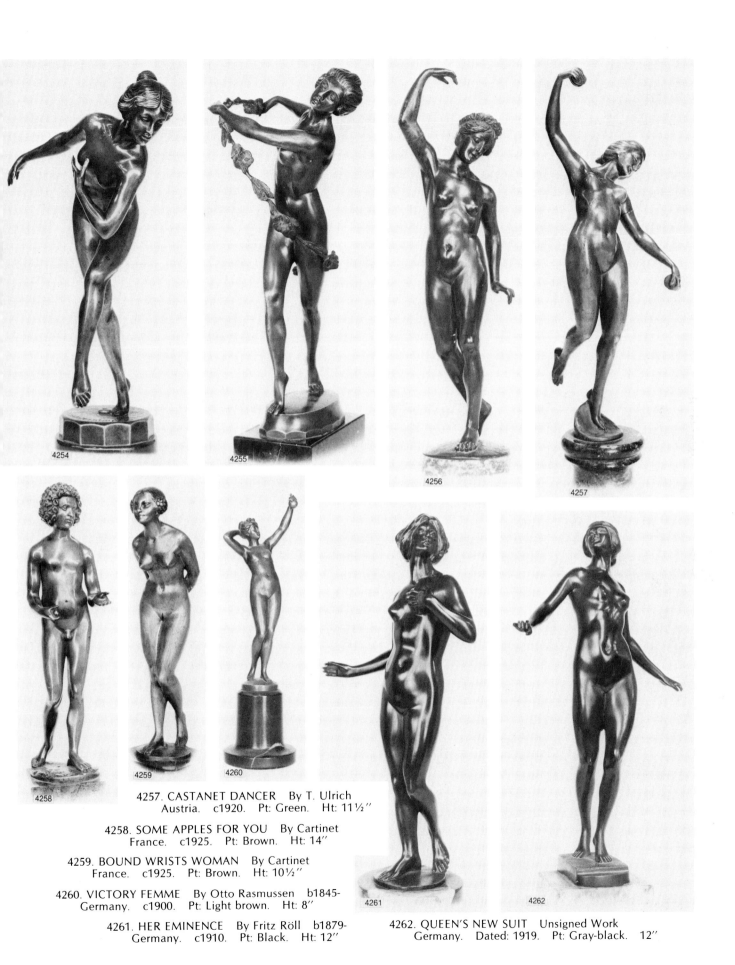

4257. CASTANET DANCER   By T. Ulrich
Austria.   c1920.   Pt: Green.   Ht: 11½″

4258. SOME APPLES FOR YOU   By Cartinet
France.   c1925.   Pt: Brown.   Ht: 14″

4259. BOUND WRISTS WOMAN   By Cartinet
France.   c1925.   Pt: Brown.   Ht: 10½″

4260. VICTORY FEMME   By Otto Rasmussen   b1845-
Germany.   c1900.   Pt: Light brown.   Ht: 8″

4261. HER EMINENCE   By Fritz Röll   b1879-
Germany.   c1910.   Pt: Black.   Ht: 12″

4262. QUEEN'S NEW SUIT   Unsigned Work
Germany.   Dated: 1919.   Pt: Gray-black.   12″

4263

4264

4265

4266

4267

4268

4270

4269

4263. EXHILARATION DANCER   Unsigned
Austria.   c1920.   Pt: Gray.   Ht: c9″

4264. THINLINE DANCER   By Lorenzl
Germany.   c1920.   Pt: Yellow.   Ht: 12″

4265. FLYING DANCER   By LeJeune
France.   c1925.   Pt: Green.   Ht: 10½″

4267. HIGH STEPPING GIRLS   By C.J.R. Colinet
France.   c1920.   Pt: Dark green.   24″

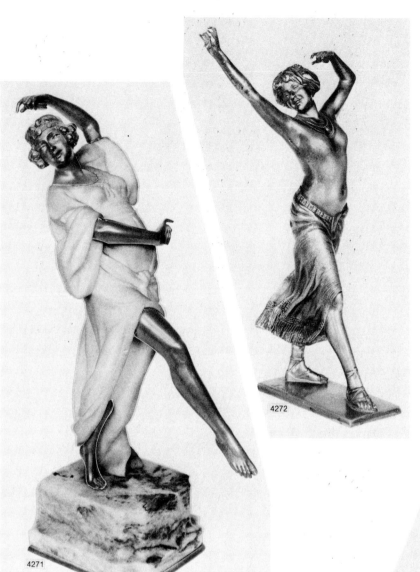

4266. SKIRTTAILS DANCER   By Lorenzl
   Germany.   c1920.   Pt: Yellow.   Ht: c7"

4268-9. UPBEAT DANCERS—Ashtray   By LeFaguays
   France.   c1925.   Pt: Yellow.   Ht: c9"

4270. NUDE DANCER   By Crefeld-Hofer
   Germany.   c1910.   Pt: Brown.   Ht: 19½"
Founder: Friedenau, Berlin.

4271. ALABASTER ROBED DANCER   By Rossi
   France.   c1920.   Pt: Brown.   Ht: 13½"

4272. HAREM DANCER   By F. Peleschka
   Austria.   c1910.   Pt: Yellow.   Ht: 7"

4273. LE VIN   By Louis Holweck/Hollweck
   France.   c1890.   Pt: Gold.   12½"   Wh.-met.
Acquired for Laville de Paris.

4274. TAMBOURINE DANCER   By R. Varnier
   France.   c1920.   Pt: Gold-bronze.   Ht: 9"

4276. SZOPHTICK   by Cartinet
   France. c1910. Pt: Green. Ht: 9½"

4277. POSING   by Schmidt-Hofer
   Germany. c1910. Yellow-brown. 12½"

4278. YELLING GIRL   by H. Keck
   Germany. c1910. Pt: Brown-green.   9½"

4279. SQUEEZING   by Ernst Seger   b1868-
   Germany. c1910. Pt: Dark brown.   10"

4280. SUNSHINE GIRL   by A. Just
   Sweden. c1930. Brown-green.   c12"

4281. SITTING   by Gino Scarpa   b1924-
   Italy. c1960. Green.   3½"   Edtn. of 8.

4283. ECHO DES BOIS
   By Henri-Honoré Plé (1853-1922)
France. c1900. Pt: Green-brown. Ht: 19½"
Musée de la Ville de Paris. Fdr: Colin, Paris.

4275. PHRYNE BEFORE THE JUDGES
By Johannes Benk   b1844-
Austria. Dated: 1907. Green-black.   9"

4285. PHRYNE DEVANT SES JUGES
By Pierre-Etienne-Daniel Campagne   b1951-
France.   c1895.   Pt: Green-brown.   Ht: 19″, 33½″
This work was also sold in alabaster.

4283

4285

4288. YOUNG HIPPY by Manzollo
Italy. c1925. Pt: Green-brown. Ht: 20"

4289. BAREFOOT GIRL by Schmidt-Felling
Germany. c1920. Pt: Brown. Ht: 7½"

4290. SEWING LADY by José Cardona
France. c1910. Pt: Dark brown. Ht: 11"

4291. SALOME Unsigned Work
France. c1910. Pt: Brown. Ht: 27"

4292. STEPPING LADY Illegible
France. c1900. Pt: Dark brown. Ht: 13"

4293. AURORE by Virgile Morez
France. c1900. Pt: Red-brown. Ht: 8½"

4294. AURORE by Hippolyte Moreau
France. c1900. Pt: Brown. Ht: 14½"

4295. BALLING by Franz Iffland
Germany. c1900. Dark brown. Ht: 13½"
Fdr: Ernst Krass, Berlin (seal).

4296. DANCER by Max Kalish b1891-
America. c1920. Pt: Dark brown. 13¼"

4286. GOODIES BASKET Unsigned Work
Germany. c1920. Pt: Dark brown. Ht: 10½"

4287. LITTLE RED Copper plate on plaster
France. c1920. Pt: Dark brown. Ht: 7½"

4291
4292
4293
4294
4295
4296
4297
4298

4297. LITTLE SHEBA   by Titze
Austria.   c1905.   Pt: Bronze.   Ht: 15″

4298. EGYPTIAN   by Victor Seifert   b1870-
Germany.   c1900.   Pt: Red-brown.   Ht: 14″

4299. PECHEUSE DANSANT
    After: Francisque-Joseph Duret   (1804-1865)
France.   c1885.   Pt: Choc.-brown. Ht: 6″ etc.

4300. MANDOLIN LADY
    By K. Hackstock   (1855-1919)
Austria.   Dated: 1918.   Brown.   11″

4301. MANDOLIN NUDE   White Metal
    By Julien Caussé   Wk: c1890-1914
France.   c1900.   Pt: Copper.   Ht: 22″

4302. DIANE WITH HORN
    By Franz Iffland   Wk: c1885-1915
Germany.   c1900.   Pt: Green-brown.   16½″

4303. GOURD SHAKE DANCER
    By Jean-Jacques Pradier   (1792-1852)
France.   c1890.   Pt: Yellow-brown.   Ht: 18″

4304. CASTANET AND TAMBOURINE
    By J.M. Picciole
France.   c1910.   Pt: Yellow.   Ht: 12″   Seal #28

    4305. TOE DANCER   Unsigned Work
        France.   c1925.   Polychrome.   Ht: 9½″

    4306. BALLERINA   by J. Loren
        Austria.   c1920.   Pt: Brown.   Ht: 6½″

    4307. FEATHER DANCER   by M. Ehledersohne
        Austria.   c1920.   Polychrome.   Ht: 9½″

4309. JEWELED ENTERTAINER
   By Schmidt-Hofer   Wk: c1900-1925
Germany.   c1920.   Pt: Gray-black.   Ht: 11½″

4310. ISADORA DUNCAN   (1878-1927)
   By Auguste Puttemans   (1866-1922)
Belgium.   Dated: 1919.   Pt: Black.   Ht: 10½″

4311. BAREFOOT DANCER
   By Rudolf Küchler   b1867-
Germany.   c1910.   Pt: Brown.   Ht: 12″

4312. PRIMA BALLERINA
   By R. Carl Bröse   b1880-
Ger./Aust.   c1910.   Pt: Brown.   Ht: 9″

4313. MOZART BOWING   Unsigned
   Austria.   c1910.   Polychrome.   Ht: c7''

4314-5. TARCHINOT AND BAULOBO
   By Emile Guillemin   (1841-1907)
France.   c1880.   Pt: Brown, gold.   Ht: 8''

4316-7. FLAMENCO DANCERS
   By Paul Aichele   Wk: c1890-1910
Germany.   Dated: 1898.   Pt: Brown-yellow.   c12''

4318. MOZART   by G. Gueylos
   France.   c1900.   Pt: Light brown.   Ht: 26''

4324   4325

4326   4327

4328

4329

4319. OBOIST   by Hofer-Cassel
    Germany.   1926.   Pt: Black.   Ht: 13½″

4320. STREET VIOLINIST   by Letton
    Germany.   c1925.   Pt: Black.   Ht: 13½″

4321. KETTLE DRUMS   by Franz Iffland
    France.   c1900.   Pt: Brown.   Ht: 4″

4322. LITTLE PIPER   Louis Kley   (1833-1911)
    France.   c1900.   Pt: Brown.   Ht: 5″

4323. HORN BLOWER   by A. Just
    Sweden.   c1935.   Pt: Brown-green.   Ht: 7″

4324-5. TOOTARES—Pair
    By Ernest Rancoulet   Wk: c1870-1915
France.   c1875.   Pt: Light brown.   Ht: 6½″
Each figure stands on signed wine-bladder.

4326-7. COURT MUSICIANS   Unsigned
    Austria.   c1900.   Pt: Brown.   Ht: 5″, 5½″

4328. CAVALIER WITH TRUMPET
    By E. Barillot
France.   c1895.   Pt: Dark brown.   Ht: 9″

4329. TROUBADOUR TOASTING
    By Ernst Geier—Fecit
Germany.   Dated: 1891.   Pt: Brown.   Ht: 5″
Fec. or Fecit is Latin for "I did it".
Many German artists used this term after their
name.

4330. STREET GUITARIST
    By V. Motzner
Hungary.   c1910.   Pt: Brown.   4½″

4331. VIOLA PLAYER 17th Century
    By Emile Picault
France.   c1900.   Pt: Brown.   27″

4332. SERENADER   Unsigned Work
    Spain.   c1910.   Green.   11½″

4333. FIVE GALLON VIOLINIST
    By Ferdinand Winkler   b1879-
Vienna.   c1910.   Light brown.   9″

4334. YOUNG VIOLIN PLAYER
    By Martin Götze   b1865-
Germany.   c1900.   Dark brown.   15½″

4335. MUSIC AND WINE   Unsigned
    France.   c1890.   Pt: Brown.   8½″

4336. BELTED PIPER   Unsigned
    France. c1920. Ivory. c7″

4337. ENCHANTED COBRA   Unsigned
    Germany. c1900. Ylo.-brown. 9″

4338. PIPERESS   by E. Hamburger   Wk: c1890-1914
    Germany. Dated: 1902. Pt: Yellow-brown. Ht: 8½″

4339. BABY PAN   Unsigned Work
    France. c1875. Pt: Yellow. Ht: 2½″

4341. MUSE DES BOIS   by Edouard Drouot (1859-1945)
    France. c1910. Pt: Gray-black. Ht: 21″   Ref: Vol. II, #1436

4343. ODE TO THE BIRDS   by Rudolf Kaesbach b1873-
    Germany. c1910. Pt: Dark brown. Ht: 8¼″

4344. SEMIRAMIS   by G. Coudray   Wk: c1883-1903
France.   c1895.   Pt: Green-brown.   23″   Seal #8

4345. SONG MERCHANT   by Paul Aichele
Germany.   c1910.   Pt: Black.   Ht: 12½″

4346. LA CIGALE   by A. Carrier-Belleuse
France.   c1875.   Brown-gold.   Ht: 15″, 19½″

4347-8. GYPSY MINSTRELS   Unsigned works
France.   c1900.   Pt: Gilded.   Ht: 17″

4350. LITTLE SHEBA   by Leo Fessler II
Germany.   c1925.   Pt: Gold.   Ht: 6½″

4351. HARP GIRL   by Ferdinand Lepcke   (1866-1909)
Germany.   Dated: 1904.   Pt: Dark green.   Ht: 12″

4347

4348

4350

4351

4353

4353. LA MUSIQUE
By Eugène Delaplanche (1836-1891)
France.   c1875.   Pt: Gold-brown.
Ht: 13½″, 22″, 26½″, 33½″, 40″, 67″
From 1896 catalogue of F. Barbedienne.

4354

4355

4355. FEMMES ET FLEURS
By Emile-Oscar Guillaume b1867-
France. c1910. Pt: Gilt. Ht: 29" W/base.
Fdr: Union de Maitres Sculpteurs.   Seal #88

Guillaume was active through the 1920's, winning
the Gold Medal (Paris) in 1924, and the honorary
title of Chevalier, 1926, an equivalent to the English
knight.

4354. JEUNE JEMME JOUANT DES CYMBALES
By Victor Joseph Segoffin   (1867-1925)
France. Dated: 1905. Pt: Green. Ht: 46" Seal #12
Founder: Susse Frères, Editors, Paris. Also chiseled in white

marble and smaller bronze editions.
Segoffin was born in Toulouse, studied under Cavelier and
Barrias. He won the Prix de Rome in 1897.

4356. FRENCH SCHOOL Boys
     By Francois-Michel Pascal   (1810-1882)
France.   c1850.   Pt: Brown.   Ht: 14½"

Pascal was student of David d'Angers. He exhibited from
1840 to 1880, children being his specialty.

4357. SCHOOL GIRL
     By Prof. Adolf Gerhard Janensch   b1860-
Germany.   Dated: 1905.   Ylo., green, brown.   22½"

Janensch was versatile rather than specialized in his subject
choice. He won the Gold Medal at the International Salon of
Berlin in 1892.

4358. THE SPINNER   by S. Schwalenberg
    Germany. c1900. Pt: Brown. Ht: 7½″

4360. GRAZIELA L'FILEUSE
    By Mathurin Moreau   (1822-1912)
    France. c1890. Pt: Yellow-brown. Ht: 21″

4361. MARGUERITE
    By Eugène Marioton   (1854-1925)
France. Dated: 1887. Pt: Brown. Ht: 24½″, 32½″
Fdr: V.F. Fiat-Lux, Paris.
Inscription: Salon des Beaux Arts 1887.

4362. UN PEU, BEAUCOUP
    Marc Christophe Douay   Wk: c1880-1900
France.   c1890.   Brown.   Ht: 28″ W/swivel base.
Title: Literally, a little, a lot. Figuratively, he loves
me, he loves me not. Volume II, #1579 miscredited,
is by Douay. See page 491 notes.

4364. BITIM DER SCHLANGE HERUNTER
    By Max Bezner   Wk: c1905-1915
France.   c1910.   Pt: Yellow-gold.   Ht: 19″
Founder: Louchet, Paris.
German born and French trained under Alfred Boucher,
Bezner exhibited from 1908 until the war, 1914.

4369

4368

4369. CARON AND POMPIER
By Auguste Nicolas Cain
(1822-1894)
France. c1860. Pt: Dark brown.

Each limier was also sold on smaller base in the above 24″ edition and two smaller ones. Caron was most popular of the two pieces.

4368. PIQUEUR AU RELAIS
By two sculptors:
Hippolyte Moreau (1832-c1917)—Man
Prosper Lecourtier (1855-1924)—Dogs
France. c1895. Pt: Dark brown.
Editions: 21″ and 31″ Seal #8
Fdr: Society of Bronzes of Paris.

Huntsman, *Piqueur* and one bloodhound, *Limier* were illustrated in Society's catalogue, c1900, titled: *Piqueur au Limier.*

4370. SCOTSMAN AND GREYHOUNDS
        France.   c1890.   Pt: Brown.   Ht: 10″
Cast in spelter with no markings.

4371. PATROL TEAM AND TRAINER
        By A. Brandel *fecit*
Polish.   c1910.   Green, brown/ivory.   7½″

4373. AU LOUP—Salon of 1888
        By Louis Auguste Hiolin   (1846-1912)
France.   Dated: 1888.   Pt: Gray-black.   31″

Exhibited, out of competition, *hors concours*, and
acquired by the state for *La Ville de Paris*. Young
shepherd and his dog in pursuit of sheep killer.
Au Loup was first shown in plaster, 1885. Last
showing was Universal Exposition of 1889, (bronze).

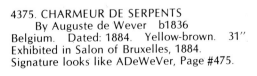

4375. CHARMEUR DE SERPENTS
By Auguste de Wever   b1836
Belgium.   Dated: 1884.   Yellow-brown.   31″
Exhibited in Salon of Bruxelles, 1884.
Signature looks like ADeWeVer, Page #475.

4376. LADY WITH COILS
By Karl Kowalczewski   b1876-
Germany.   Dated: 1908.   Pt: Brown.   Ht: 11½″

4377. SNAKE DANCER   By Nam Greb—Bergman
Vienna, Austria.   c1910.   Brown.   8½″

4378. JARDINIERE FEE AUX LEZARDS
By Louis Ernest Barrias   (1841-1905)
France.   c1896.   Pt: Gold-doré.   Ht: 8½″
In Barbedienne catalogue, 1886, at 55fr.

4379. CHARMEUSE DE SERPENTS
By Edouard Drouot   (1859-1945)
France.   c1920.   Pt: Green-brown.   Ht: 27″

4380-1. EGYPTIAN SNAKE HOLDERS   Unsigned
Austria.   c1900.   Pt: Brown.   Ht: c7″

4383. MODERN EVE
By Robert Toberentz   (1849-1895)
America.   Dated: 1887.   Pt: Brown.   Ht: 38″
Fdr: Henry Bonnard Bronze Co. N.Y. 1898.

This casting would have been completed, 1898.
Dates signed with sculptor's name note year of his
creation and is unchanged through decades of
commercial casting. Toberentz of Berlin has works
conserved in Berlin, Hambourg, and Köln museums.

4384
4385
4386
4387
4388
4389

4384. ITALIAN CLOWN—Lady by Vincent-Désiré Faure de Broussé
France. c1890. Pt: Gold bronze. Ht: 24½″

4385. HARLEQUIN MASQUERADER—Lady   by Emile LaPorte   (1858-1907)
France.   c1900.   Pt: Yellow-brown.   Ht: 21″   Fdr: Gadaix.

4386. LAW AND THE DEAD RABBIT   by Chenier
France.   c1890.   Pt: Yellow-brown.   Ht: 24½″

4387. MINUET IN "A" FLAT   by Clement Leopold Steiner   (1853-1899)
France.   c1890.   Pt: Yellow-brown.   Ht: 25″

4388-9. CIRCUS BUFFOONS—Equestrian   Unsigned Set
France.   c1890.   Pt: Brown-black.   Ht: c20″
Alternate pairs have signature, A. Barye and A.B.

4390. CALLING GIRL—On Her Toes   by Alfred Grevin   (1827-1892)
France.   c1880.   Pt: Yellow-brown.   Ht: 19½″   Fdr: E. Tassel.

4391. HISTOIRE—Modele Sans Draperies
By Alfred Boucher (1850-1934)
France.   c1903.   Pt: Yellow-black.   Ht: 19″, 25½″, 33″
Fdr: Siot-Decauville, Paris. Also done in draped version.

4392. LISTENING GIRL—On Stone Perch   by Pierre Andrée
France.   c1910.   Pt: Green-brown.   Ht: 22″

4393. RUSALKA—The Little Mermaid   by Frank James Morgan
America.   c1976.   Cold cast bronze, green.   Ht: 42″
Sculptor and founder, Morgan, won Gold Medal, National Sculpture
Society, New York, 1977.

4396

THE TIDE

Translated loosely, from an old Dutch boobimyser.

The fickle, undulating Tide approaches the Shore which is eager for her teasing swells. She arrives in a great swoop and he holds her—but does he? No she slips away, leaving as though she were still advancing—yet farther she slips from the Shore. Gone, she is gone to some distant shore repeating her acts of indecision. But while you sleep, she is returning anew—for this Shore is Hers to devastate routinely—to conquer some day.
Anon.

4395

4395. INDIAN LOVERS—The Fugitives by Désiré-Pierre-Louis Marie France. c1865. Pt: Red-brown. Ht: 17½″ Fdr: Delafontaine et Saulo, Paris. Lovers from hostile tribes in sinking raft. Temporary haven is middle of wide Missouri—Legend.

4396. THE TIDE AND THE SHORE
Johannes Uhde (1850-1908)
Ger. Dated: 1886. Green. 17½″
Fdr: Guss. Bierling, Dresden.

4397. UN SECRET—Medal au Salon
   By Hippolyte Moreau   b1832-
France.   c1905.   Pt: Brown.   Ht: 21″
Green, white and black marble, 1″, has fitted and
beveled, bronze underplate—a deluxe touch to any
bronze.

4399. THE KISS
   By Ferdinand Lepcke   (1866-1909)
Germany.   c1900.   Pt: Mottled green. Ht: 23″
Fdr: Buss. Martin u. Piltzing, Berlin.

4403. FLEURS DE PRINTEMPS
Gustave Frederic Michel   (1851-1924)
Fr.   1889.   Pt: Brn.   Ht: 39''   Seals #89, 90

Medaille d'Or winner—adapted later for lamp.
Overall detail, knurled skin texture and soft
deep brown patina give lifelike appearance to
Flowers of Springtime.

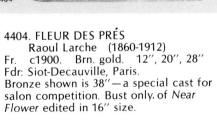

4404. FLEUR DES PRÉS
   Raoul Larche   (1860-1912)
Fr.   c1900.   Brn. gold.   12″, 20″, 28″
Fdr: Siot-Decauville, Paris.
Bronze shown is 38″—a special cast for
salon competition. Bust only, of *Near
Flower* edited in 16″ size.

4405. CUPID AND PSYCHE
   Mathurin Moreau   (1822-1912)
France.   c1875.   Brown-green.   32″

Fine work on this complicated (eighteen-
piece) casting indicates its probable use
as a competition piece. Oval base was
designed for a three to six inch marble
base—optional.

4406

4407

4407. LE PLAISIR—Delighted
By Claudius Marioton   (1844-1919)
France.   c1880.   Pt: Dark brown.   Ht: 27″

4406. AMOUR CAPTIF
Felix Sanzel   (1829-1883)
France.   c1870.   Pt: Brown tones.   Ht: 31″

4408

4409

4410

4408. GOURMANDE   Raoul Larche (1860-1912)
    France.   c1900.   Pt: Red-brown.   Ht: 17½″
Edited by both Siot-D. and Colin Cie., Paris.
Title: *Greedy Glutton*—Miss Gourmande won't share
her load of grapes with a hungry goat.

4409. PETIT ROI—Little King of Hearts
    By Raoul Larche   (1860-1912)
    France.   c1900.   Pt: Brown.   Ht: 12″   Rock 4″
Fdr: Siot-Decauville, Paris. Also in doré patina.

4410. FAUNE A LA TORTUE—Faun and Tortoise
    By Edouard Drouot   (1859-1945)
    France.   c1910.   Pt: Brown.   Ht: 13″, *17″*, 23″

4412. MUSIQUE by Eugène Marioton (1854-1925)
France. c1900. Pt: Green-brown. Ht. 24"
Founder: E. Collin et Cie., Paris.

4413. SONG OF THE SEA—Volume IV Cover Girl
By Mathurin Moreau (1822-1912)
France. Dated: 1904. Pt: Green, gold. Ht: 32"
Fdr: Copyright by Lapointe, Paris.
Has swivel base, 360°, and concave medal of honor
seal. Lamp fixture is removable. Edited in several
sizes up to four feet.

4414. FÉE DES BOIS—The Bird Fairy
By Eutrope Bouret (1833-1906)
France. c1875. Pt: Gray. Ht: 22½"
Fee des Bois—gentlest of the sprites.

4415. FÉE AUX FLEURS—The Flower Fairy
By Eugène Delaplanche (1836-1891)
France. c1875. Pt: Brown-black. Ht: 24½"
Fdr: Ferdinand Barbedienne, Paris.

4416. NYMPHE AL ECHO
By Manture
France. c1890.
Pt: Gray-blk. Ht: 19½"
Plaque: Par Eleve de
l'Ecole des Beaux
Arts—by a student of
the Fine Arts School.

4419. DEPART DES MIRONDELLES
By Auguste Moreau   Wk: c1860-1910
France.   c1890.   Pt: Dark brown.   Ht: 33½''
Green marble base w/plaque, 3½'', diameter 10''

4420. ÉTOILE DU MATIN—The Morning Star
By Adrien Etienne Gaudez   (1845-1902)
France.   c1890.   Pt: Dark brown.   Ht: 23'', 35''
This *Star* watches over fauna and flora, both seen on
hemisphere base.

4418. ÉTOILE D'AMOUR—Star of Love
By Alfred-Jean Foretay   b1861-
France.   c1890.   Pt: Dark brown.   Ht: 50''

4421. L'AURORE—
    Goddess of the Dawn, Awakening
    By Jean Verschnieder   Wk: c1900-1915
France.   c1910.   Pt: Silver wash.   Ht: 23½″
Design is adaptable for a suspended timepiece.

4422. LUMIÈRE POUR L'NAVIGATEUR
    By Jean Baptist Germain   Wk: c1865-1910
France.   c1900.   Pt: Brown.   Ht: 25″, 35″
Light for the Sailor in smaller edition had different
title. All sizes originally had marble bases.

4424. ANGEL OF INDUSTRY
    By George Charles Coudray   Wk: c1883-1903
France.   c1895.   Pt: Dark brown.   Ht: 34″
Angel is appropriately proportioned to represent the
newly harnessed power of electricity.

4426. HIRONDELLE DE MER—The Sea Swallow
By Jean Baptiste Germain (c1845-1910)
France. c1900. Pt: Green-brown. Ht: 36″ Seal #18

4426

4428

4428. ÉTOILE DU BERGER—
    Star of the Shepherd
    By Hippolyte Moreau   Wk: c1889-1917
France.   c1895.   Pt: Dark brown.
Ht: 29″, 37″   Seal #8
Founder: Société des Bronzes de Paris.

4429. PAPILLON—Psyche or Butterfly or Soul
    By Franz Rosse   (1858-1900)
    Germany.   Dated: 1890.   Pt: Brown.   Ht: 14″

4430. FÉE DE PRINTEMPS—Spirit of Spring
    By Mathurin Moreau   (1822-1912)
    France.   c1865.   Pt: Dark brown.   Ht: 31½″

4432. FÉE ET LA SOURCE   by Mathurin Moreau
    France.   Salon: 1876.   Pt: Brown-black.   Ht: 27″

4433. LA SOURCE—Med d'Or   Wh.-Metal
   By Louis Auguste Moreau   (1855-1919)
France. c1890.   Pt: Brown.   Ht: 7½"   Marble ½"

4434. GRANTOR OF WISHES   by P.L. Kowalczewski
   Germany.   c1900.   Pt: Yellow-brown.   Ht: 8½"

4435. ICARUS—Son of Daedalus   Unsigned
   Austria.   Dated: 1899.   Pt: Green.   Ht: 7"

4436. MOON BAT-GIRL   by Oswalt Schimmelfennig
   Germany.   Dated: 1897.   Pt: Yellow.   Ht: 17"

4437. INSECT DANCER   by Barner
   Austria.   c1910.   Pt: Yellow-black.   Ht: 8"

4438. ANGEL OF GLORY   by J. Sonzowacht
   Ger.   c1915.   Pt: Gray.   Ht: 18"   Wh.-metal

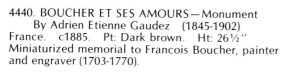

4440. BOUCHER ET SES AMOURS—Monument
By Adrien Etienne Gaudez   (1845-1902)
France.   c1885.   Pt: Dark brown.   Ht: 26½''
Miniaturized memorial to Francois Boucher, painter
and engraver (1703-1770).

4441-2. FAIRIES OF LIGHT AND FIRE   Unsigned
France.   c1875.   Pt: Dark brown.   Ht: 18½''

4443. EAGLE AND THE SOURCE
By Louis-Charles-Hip. Buhot   (1815-1865)
France.   c1860.   Pt: Yellow-brown.   Ht: c24''

4445. ÉTOILE DES HIRONDELLES
    By Adrien Etienne Gaudez   (1845-1902)
France.   c1885.   Pt: Green.   Ht: 27″, 38½″

One *Star* and six swallows can be counted. Original marble or bronze second base added stability and about four inches to height.

4446. LA FÉE DES MERS—Fairy of the Seas
    By Luca Madrassi   (c1869-1914)
France.   c1895.   Pt: Brown, yellow.   Ht: 23″, 39″

Rim below sea shell has nub which fits into lower swivel base. Worn patina on end of shell indicates it has been used as a handle through the years.

4447

4448

4447. TROIS TÊTES DE FEMMES
   By Albert Ernest Carrier-Belleuse (1824-1887)
France. c1865. Pt: Yellow-gold. Ht: 35″

Three Wild Women was executed for the lobby of
Hotel de Paiva, Champs-Elysees a Paris (annee 1865).
Nicely balanced views appear as bronze is turned a
full 360°. Original, multi contoured red-marble
weighed more than the bronze.

4448. GIRL MOVED BY TWO LOVES
   By Luca Madrassi (c1869-1914)
France. c1899. Pt: Mottled brown. Ht: 28½″

Madrassi was master of the fantastic. Fairies, cupids,
sprites, angels, bacchantes, satyrs and genies, etc.
were his favorite subjects. The *Fée des Mers* and
#4448 are typical of his great imagination.

4450. INQUISITIVE LOVE
     By Mathurin Moreau   (1822-1912)
France.   c1890.   Pt: Natural yellow.   Ht: 27″

Natural yellow looks much like gold and can be buffed and
lacquered. Pieces with no finish may have been sold like this
or stripped of whatever patina (finish) they originally had.
They should not be confused with gilt or doré.

4451. LES TROIS AMIS—Hors Concours
     By Mathurin Moreau   (1822-1912)
     France.   c1895.   Pt: Brown and yellow.   Ht: 23½″
     Water flows over elegant white, red and black marble 2″.

4449. LA BAIGNEUSE—The Bather   White Metal
     Fdr: Miroy Frères a Paris
France.   Dated: 1881.   Pt: Dark brown.   Ht: 30″

4452. BEAUTE SANS EGAL
    By Auguste Moreau   Wk: c1860-1910
France.   c1875.   Pt: Brown.   Ht: 24''
Fdr: J. Chardon et Petit Fils, 21-23 Rue des Filles du
Calvaire, Paris.

Master founder Chardon is active and can still do a
superior job on 'Beaute' from his original one hundred
year old molds (sand casting).

4453. SHARING THE WELL
    By Mathurin Moreau   (1822-1912)
France.   c1870.   Pt: Brown and oxidized green.
Fdr: Susse Frères, Paris.   Ht: 25''

A rare and very fine subject. Contrasting patinization
must be seen to be appreciated.

4454

4455

4454. WAITING FOR THE BOATS—Medal of Honor
By Mathurin Moreau   (1822-1912)
France.   c1905.   Pt: Brown tones.   Ht: 38″

Has convex Medaille d'Honneur seal and was
exhibited *hors concours*. Cast in two smaller editions.

4455. RETOUR DE MOISSON—Return from Harvest
By Mathurin Moreau   (1822-1912)
France.   c1890.   Pt: Green-brown.   Ht: 26½″, 34″
Fdr: Ancne. Maison Colin, Paris. Sold by Tiffany, N.Y.

Catalog of about 1910 (Colin) shows companion
piece titled, *Retour de Vendange* (Return from Grape
Gathering), in same sizes. Girl and smaller boy are
loaded with grapes. Catalog does not show the
bronzes with any bases. These could be chosen from
stock examples or cut to order.

4456. A SECRET CONFIDENCE
By A. Carrier-Belleuse   (1824-1887)
France.   c1880.   Pt: Dark brown.   Ht: 32"

4459. RETOUR DES CUEILLEUSES
By Hippolyte Moreau   (1832-c1917)
France.   Dated: 1882.   Pt: Brown.   Ht: 29"

Red antique marble 5". Marble swivels on special wood pedestal.
Inscribed: Salon des Beaux Arts.

4460

4461

4460. BERGERS D'ARCADIE
    By Eugène-Antoine Aizelin   (1821-1902)
France.   Dated: 1867.   Pt: Natural bronze.
Fdr: F. Barbedienne, Paris.   Ht: 12″, 20″, 24″, 41″

Title means any simple, rural shepherds. Word
Arcadie refers to a pastoral province of Greece.

4461. SPRING AND SUMMER
    By Henri-Etienne Dumaige   (1830-1888)
France.   c1875.   Pt: Yellow-green.   Ht: 14″
Summer can often solve the problems of *Spring*.

4462-3. THE LAND AND THE SEA
    By Henri-Etienne Dumaige   (1830-1888)
France.   Dated: 1872.   Pt: Gold-brown.   Ht: 19″
Special 4″ wood decorator bases were made for
Marshall Field and Co. to augment this pair.

4464. L'PAPILLON—Lady with Butterfly
By Emile Louis Picault   born 1839-
France.   c1880.   Pt: Brown.   Ht: 17"

Black slate base 1½". Note signature on rim. This piece is atypical of Picault's strong featured men. He shows less versatility in later years because his reputation prospered on a strong male type.

4462

4463

4464

4467. LA MOISSON
   The Harvest Dance
By Didier Debut   (1824-1893)
Fr.   1884.   Brown.   30″

4467

LA MOISSON

4469. PERRETTE
    By Eugène Aizelin   (1821-1902)
France.   c1875.   Pt: Brown.   Ht: 30″
One of a dozen seated girl and boy
subjects by Eugène Aizelin.

4471. MARGUERITE A L'EGLISE — In Church
    Lefevre-Deslongchamps   (1849-1893)
France.   c1890.   Pt: Dark brn.   Ht: 18″
Exhibited in salons of 1877, 1878, 1889.
Conserved at Museum of Cherbourg, Fr.

4472-3. PEASANT COUPLE
    By Albert Cheuret
France.   c1910.   Pt: Green.   Ht: 13½″

4474. ANDALOUSE   by Antoine Bofill   Wk: c1885-1915
France.   c1910.   Pt: Doré/ivory.   Ht: 16″

4475. ANDALOUSE   by A. Rossetto
Italy.   c1910.   Pt: Brown.   H12″   Seal #41

4476. MADRIDIAN MODEL   by Bruno Zack
Germany.   c1920.   Pt: Polychrome.   Ht: 9½″

4477. UPPER CLASS LADY   by Beneliare
Italy.   c1920.   Pt: Brown-green.   Ht: 10½″

4478. LADY IN REPOSE—Half Figure
By Pierre (Prince) Troubetzkoy   b1864-
America.   Dated: 1923.   Pt: Dark brown.   Ht: 12½″

4479. MOON MAID
    Julien Caussé   Wk: c1890-1914
France.   c1905.   Pt: Brown.   19″, 29″

4481. DAYDREAMS
    By Paul Gasq   (1860-1944)
France.   c1900.   Dark brown.   34½″

4485. PAQUERETTE — The Daisy
By Adrien-Etienne Gaudez (1845-1902)
France. c1890. Pt: Dark brown. Ht: 17½″
Title is French nickname for *Little Margaret.*

4484. JOLI COUSEUSE — Sewing Charmer
By Eugène-Antoine Aizelin (1821-1902)
France. c1880. Pt: Gold-doré. Ht: 16″

4483. POSTE RESTANTE — Aux Champs
By C. Anfrie   Wk: c1880-1915
France. c1890. Pt: Dark brown. Ht: 15″
Trans: *Post office of the Birds Nest* — A secret place
to exchange love letters.

4486. GATHERER OF FLOWERS
By Henri Giraud   Wk: c1870-1895
France.   c1890.   Pt: Golden.   Ht: 13"

4487. REBECCA TRISTE
By Jean Baptiste Germain   (c1845-1910)
France.   c1890.   Pt: Golden.   Ht: 25½"

4489. MIMI—La Boheme, 1896, by Puccini
By Henri Honoré Plé   (1853-1922)
France.   c1900.   Pt: Yellow-gold.   Ht: 25"
Much of Ple's work up to 1900 shows a strong
influence of his teacher, Mathurin Moreau. *Mimi* is
such a case.

4492

4495

4492. MARIE ANTOINETTE—Guillotine Bound
   By Lord Ronald Sutherland Gower   (c1845-1915)
France.   Dated: 1876.   Pt: Brown.   Ht: 46''
Sold at Tiffany and Co. N.Y. Also done in bust.

4495. LA JEUNESSE—The Young Lady
   By Henri-Michel-Antoine Chapu   (1833-1891)
France.   c1880.   Pt: Dark brown.   Ht: 46½''
Fdr: F. Barbedienne, Paris. Editions: 23½'', 37½''

The original marble, displayed in the Paris Salon of
1875, catalogue #2940, is still on display in the patio
of the Beaux-Arts school in Paris. *Est au monument
d'Henri Regnault*, from his students, by Chapu.
Copies are in several museums. This is his most
popular work.

4496. MESSAGE OF THE BIRDS
     15th Century Lady
Henri-Honoré Plé   (1853-1922)
France.   c1900.   Pt: Silver, red,
shades of brown and gold.   Ht: 31",
Black marble with bronze trim 2", is
fitted with a swivel.

This masterwork in drapery and cloth
design has special multi-color
patinization. Gold application on
gown gives illusion of transparency to
the cloth. We count five silver birds.

1125

4497

4498

4497. PÊCHEUSE
   By Eugène Laurent   (c1832-1898)
France.   c1880.   Pt: Dark brown.   Ht: 26″
Fdr: Bisson and Ribot, Fabricants Editeurs,
Bronzes d'Art. Smaller sizes: 12″, 17½″, 22″.

Laurent's most famous works are monuments
to Francois Boucher and Jacques Callot.

4498. ANDROMEDA—Captive of the Sea
   By Adrien Etienne Gaudez   (1845-1902)
France.   c1890.   Pt: Gold, green.   Ht: 23″

Gaudez's early career was interrupted while a prisoner
of Germans in 1870-1871. He studied under Jouffroy.
Gaudez did some art nouveau as seen here, but quickly
returned to a classic realism that served him well.

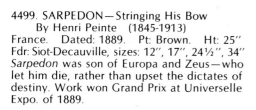

4499. SARPEDON—Stringing His Bow
   By Henri Peinte   (1845-1913)
France.   Dated: 1889.   Pt: Brown.   Ht: 25"
Fdr: Siot-Decauville, sizes: 12", 17", 24½", 34"
Sarpedon was son of Europa and Zeus—who
let him die, rather than upset the dictates of
destiny. Work won Grand Prix at Universelle
Expo. of 1889.

4500. LE FAUCHEUR—The Mower
   By Paul M.L. Richer   (1849-1933)
France.   c1880.   Pt: Brown.   Ht: 13½", 22"
Founder: Goldschieder, Paris. Seal #38
Original work is conserved at Museum of Chartres.

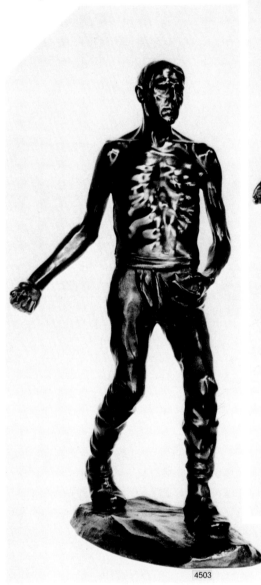

4504

4503

4502

4502. NEUE SAAT—The Sower
    By Adolf Jahn   b1858-
Germany.   Dated: 1917.   Pt: Brown.   Ht: 31½″

4503. SEEDING THE LAND   by A. Joust
    Sweden.   c1900.   Pt: Gray-black.   Ht: 25½″

4504. LADY SOWER
    By Müller-Crefeld, Berlin   b1863-
Germany.   c1919.   Pt: Light brown.   Ht: 14½″

4514

4512

4513

4515

4516

4516. WATER GIRL   by Karl Kowalczewski   b1876-
Germany.   c1910.   Green, brown, yellow.   12″, *15″*, 18″

4517. RESTING FARM GIRL   by P. Tereszczuk
Austria.   c1910.   Pt: Brown.   Ht: 4½"

4518. RAKE GIRL   Unsigned work
Austria.   c1910.   Pt: Brown tones.   Ht: 9"

4519.   GLEANER   by P.L. Kowalczewski   b1876-
Germany.   c1910.   Pt: Green-brown.   Ht: 9½"
Alternate title: *Das Mädchen Bauer*

4520. MOISSONNEUSE—Harvester
By Edouard Drouot   (1859-1945)
France.   c1910.   Pt: Dark brown.   Ht: 10"
Exposition des Beaux-Arts.   Seal #91, Pinedo.

4521. FANEUSE—Haymaker
By Antoine Bofill   Wk: c1885-1925
France.   c1910.   Pt: Brown.   Ht: 14½"   Seal #22

4522. WHEELBARROW—Inkwell Design
    By P. Tereszczuk
Austria.   c1900.   Yellow-brown.   Ht: 5½'' X 9''

4523. WHEELBARROW AND PICKAX
    By Emile Nestor Carlier   (1849-1927)
France.   c1910.   Pt: Brown.   Ht: 6¼''

4524. THE QUARRYMAN—Marble Mover
    By Edouard Drouot   (1859-1945)
France.   c1910.   Pt: Dark brown.   Ht: c9''

4525. THE QUARRY WORKER—Loader
    By Edouard Drouot   (1859-1945)
France. c1910.   Pt: Green-brown.   Ht: 10½''
Guaranteed (Vrai) bronze, seal #27.

4526

4527

4528

4529

4526. WILLIAM SHAKESPEARE   1564-1616
　　Unsigned work
England.　c1890.　Pt: Black.　Ht: 6½"

4527. JOHN BURROUGHS   1837-1921
　　Unsigned—Bronze over plaster
American.　c1925.　Pt: Brown.　Ht: 6¼"

4528. IMMORTALITY—Glory of Labor
　　Copyright, Christofle of Paris
France.　c1900.　Pt: Silver.　Ht: 15½"

4529. SHEARING TIME
　　By Jean Gautherin　(1840-1890)
France.　c1890.　Pt: Silver.　Ht: 12"
Sold by Christofle & Cie., Paris.

4530

4532

4533

4534

4530. VELLEDA—Germanic Legend
Hippolyte Maindron   (1801-1884)
France.   c1850.   Pt: Yellow.   Ht: 18″

Her rare virginity was saved by becoming a
moth. See Velleda moth.
Original marble version, from master plaster
(1839), shown in Salon of 1844. Placed in
Jardin du Luxembourg. Edited by Tiptoz
Bronzier, Paris, in three sizes.

4532. JEUNE FILLE DE BOU-SAADA
L. Ernest Barrias   (1841-1905)
France.   c1980.   Pt: Doré.   13″   Seal #12

Original bronze seen at 1890 Salon
competition. Later displayed at 1900
Exposition Centennale. Placed in *Musée du
Marseille* 1907. Edited in several sizes and
patinas by Susse Frères of Paris. Bust made
from this piece is in Volume III, #2415

4533-4. FARMER AND WIFE
By Alfred J.B. Halou   b1829-
France.   c1860.   Dark brown.   Ht: 16½″

4535

4536

4537

4541

4538

4539

4540

4535. FARM TRANQUILLITY   Unsigned work
    Austria.   c1910.   Depatined.   Ht: 5½″

4536. PLOW HORSE AND FARMER
    By Schmidt-Felling   Wk: c1895-1930
Germany.   c1910.   Pt: Brown.   Ht: 8″

4542

4543

4544

4545

4537. ROMANIAN SHEPHERD SCENE
   By Lanyi   1922
Romania.   Dated: 1922.   Pt: Dk. brown.   Ht: 16″

4538. SHEPHERD IN SUMMER   by O. Hoffman
   Germany.   c1910.   Pt: Brown.   Ht: 11½″

4539. WATER BOY   by Chinrozzi, Naples.
   Italy.   c1925.   Pt: Green-gold.   Ht: 9½″

4540. BEARDED MAN   by E. Thomasson
   Holland.   c1910.   Pt: Gold-brown.   Ht: 12″

4541. NATURE BOY
   By Hans Weddo von Glümer   b1867-
Germany.   Dated: 1892.   Pt: Brown.   Ht: 11″

4542. PLOWING   Unsigned/Iron Casting
   Russian.   c1880.   Pt: Black.   Ht: 9½″

4543. SHEPHERD SERENITY
   By Andreas Ruff   b1885-
Austria.   c1910.   Pt: Brown.   Ht: 9″

4544. FANEUSE POUR ÉTALON
   By Albert-Lefeuvre   Wk: c1875-1913
France. c1905. Pt: Green-brown.   Ht: 19½"

4545. BULL AND HEIFER
   By Isidore Bonheur (1827-1909)
France. c1880. Pt: Brown.   Ht: 12", 19"
Also cast as pair on small bases.

4546. SCHWEIN   Unsigned
   Ger. or Fr. c1900.   Black.   4½"

4547. NEW GENERATION
   By Germaine-Ourg
France. c1925. Grn.-brown.   Ht: 14½"
Founder: Etling, Paris.

4548. STUBBORN PIG — Nogo Sloham
   Johann-Robert Korn (1873-1921)
Ger.   Dated: 1908. Pt: Black.   Ht: 8½"
Prize, Exposition of Berlin, 1909.

4550. KNITTER AND NIBBLER
By Isidore Bonheur (1827-1909)
France. c1880. Pt: Red-brown. 12½"
Modern casts available from active Parisian
founder using old molds.

4552. MOTHER CHILD AND COW
Erich Schmidt-Kestner b1877-
Germany. c1910. Pt: Brown. Ht: 14½"

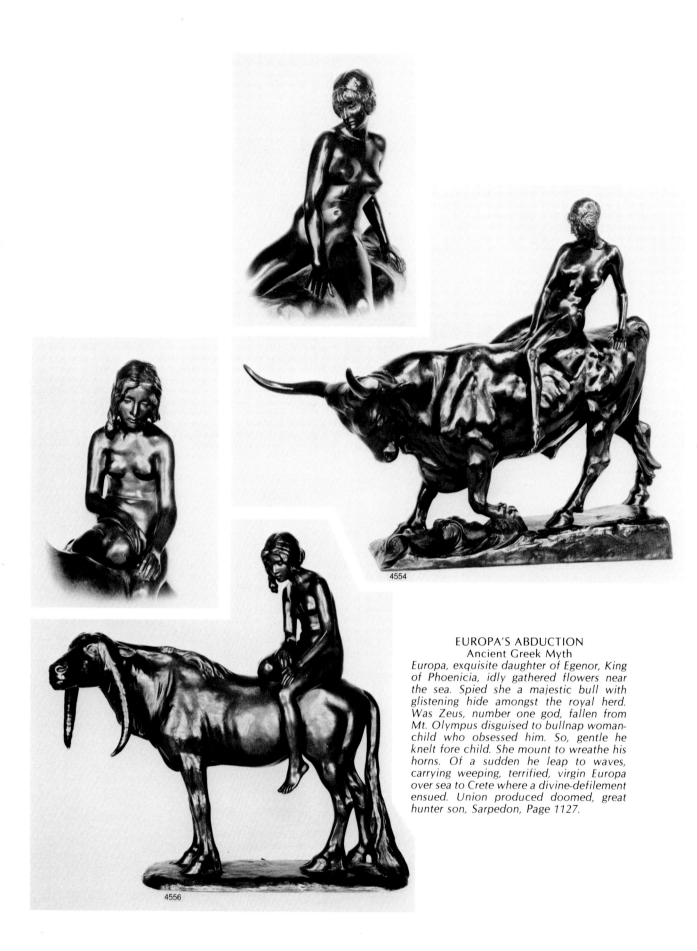

4554

4556

EUROPA'S ABDUCTION
Ancient Greek Myth

Europa, exquisite daughter of Egenor, King of Phoenicia, idly gathered flowers near the sea. Spied she a majestic bull with glistening hide amongst the royal herd. Was Zeus, number one god, fallen from Mt. Olympus disguised to bullnap woman-child who obsessed him. So, gentle he knelt fore child. She mount to wreathe his horns. Of a sudden he leap to waves, carrying weeping, terrified, virgin Europa over sea to Crete where a divine-defilement ensued. Union produced doomed, great hunter son, Sarpedon, Page 1127.

1140

4554. RAPE OF EUROPA
    Albert Hussmann b1874-
Ger. c1910. Dark brown. Ht: 19″
Monogram: E.N.

4556. EUROPA'S THEME—Musk Ox
    Hermann Haase-Ilsenburg b1879-
Germany. 1903. Pt: Brown. Ht: 16″
Founder: Oskar Gladenbeck, Berlin.

4557. TWO BY THE EAR
    By Paul Mauske b1871-
Germany. Dated: 1919. Brown. Ht: 12½″
Fdr: H. Noack Friedenaw, Berlin.

4559. PENSIVE HARMONIA ON MOOSE
    By Hermann Haase-Ilsenburg b1879-
Germany. c1906. Dark brown. Ht: 15½″
Monogram: N.W.

4561. MONUMENT TO FAME   by Carl Kauba
      Austria. c1895. Red-brown. Ht: 33¼"

4562. VERITAS—Reflections of Truth
      By Carl Kauba (1865-1922)
Austria. c1900. Yellow, brown, green. 10½"

4563. LAZY LOVERS   by Carl Kauba
      Austria. c1900. Pt: Gold. Ht: 7¼"

4564

WAGNER

4565

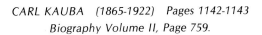

4566

H ALL MY BEST WISHES

4567

CARL KAUBA   (1865-1922)   Pages 1142-1143
Biography Volume II, Page 759.

4564. HUNTERS' PRIZE   by Carl Kauba
   Austria.   c1910.   Pt: Polychromed.   Ht: 6½" X 14½"

4565. WILHELM WAGNER   1813-1883   by C. Kauba
   Austria.   c1910.   Pt: Brown.   Ht: c8"
German composer: Flying Dutchman, Tannhauser,
Lohengrin, Tristan und Isolde, etc.

4566. LUDWIG VAN BEETHOVEN   1770-1827   by C. Kauba
   Austria.   c1910.   Pt: Dark brown.   Ht: 8¼"
German born, moved to Vienna at age Twenty-two. He was
first of the romantic composers.

4567. WARM HOSPITALITY
   By Carl Kauba   (1865-1922)
Austria.   c1900.   Pt: Ylo.-brown.   Ht: 13"
Color of 2" marble base varied—but not
dimensions. Plaque was special order.

4569. GOOD NIGHT GIRL
  Bessie Potter-Vonnoh
  (1872-1955)
Amer. c1930. Dk.-brown. 10½"
Fdr: Roman Bronze Works, N.Y.
American school impressionist style. Illusion of eyes is created by darkened patina in recessed cavities.

4570. IMAGE OF BEAUTY
  By Brenda Putnam
  (1890-1962)
Amer. c1930. Red-brown. 15"
Fdr: Kunst Foundry, N.Y.
American late-impressionist style. Darkness in recessed cavities give illusion of eyes. She is most famous for her portrait busts.

4571. DAINTY STEPS
  Bessie Potter-Vonnoh
  (1872-1955)
Amer. c1925. Pt: Black. 17¼"
Fdr: Roman Bronze Works, N.Y.

4573

4574

S·Gertrud

4575

4576

4572. CALL OF THE SEA   by Charles Leonard Hartwell
    England. c1909. Pt: Dark brown. Ht: 18½"
*Inscription: The rolling mist came down and hid the land and never
home came she. The Western Wind was wild with foam and all alone
went she. From Call of the Sea by Charles Kongeley.*

4573. SAINT JOAN   by Maurice Dellanoy   b1885-
    France. c1930. Pt: Brown tones. Ht: 14½"

4574. SAINT BARBARA   by Richard Gurbe
    America. Dated: 1904. Pt: Dark brown. Ht: 18"

4575. SAINT GERTRUD   by Ferdinand Hartzer   (1838-1906)
    Germany. c1890. Pt: Dark brown. Ht: 15"
Founder: Guss. v. W. & P. Gladenbeck, Berlin

4576. ATHENA—Goddess of Wisdom, Skills and Warfare
    By Paul Marcel Dammann   (1885-1939)
France. Dated: 1919. Pt: Brown. Diameter: 4½"
*Reverse: Association Desécrivains Combattants 1914-1919. A notre
Emmanuel Bourcier.* War correspondents' award.

4577. DIANE Signed, Glazed Pottery
France. c1925. Purple-brown. c13″

4578. NYMPH AND DEER
By Alexandre Morlon b1878-
France. 1926. Green-brown. 14″ x 31″
Medal of Honor Seal #91.

4579. NATIONAL PRIDE by Ouline
France. c1933. Green. Ht: 13½″

4581

4582

4583

4580. DIANE AND HOUNDS
Rudolf Kaesbach   b1873-
Germany.   c1920.   Black.   Ht: 21½"

Kaesbach's work was cast in Paris,
Düsseldorf, Brussels und Antwerpen.
Many of his subjects show mythological
influence.

4581. THE AVIATOR
Alfred Gilbert   (1854-1934)
France.   c1925.   Green.   Ht: 16½"

4582. GODDESS OF THE HUNT
By A. Lavaysse
France.   c1928.   Green-brown.   19½"
Carries Lost-wax seal on base.

4583. WOODLAND SCENE
Pierre Octave Vigoureux   b1884
France.   c1930.   Pt: Brown.   Ht: 25"
Carries *Lastele* seal #55, Paris.

4584

4585

4587

4588

4584. SUN GODDESS—Ten Steps   Unsigned
    France. c1923. Pt: Brown.   Ht: 7½"
Ten layer, red marble base, 8½"

4585. ODE TO A DOE
    By Ary Jean-Léon Bitter   (1883-1960)
France. c1930. Brown. Ht: 11½" x 26"
Fdr: Susse Frères, Cire-perdue.   Seal #72

4587. UNTOUCHABLE NYMPH
    By Pierre LeFaguays   Wk: c1920-1935
France. 1927. Pt: Brown-green.   Ht: 22"

4588. MUSICAL SATYR
      Auguste Gilbert Private   (1892-1970)
France.   c1935.   Pt: Dark green.   Ht: 21″
Fdr: Susse Frères—Cire-perdue, Paris.

      4589. FLEET GAZELLES   by Fayral
            France.   c1930.   Green.   9 x 26″
Fdr: Leverrier of Paris.   Seal #61

This company was a white-metal specialist.
Their sculptures often pass for bronze.

      4590. SIBLING RIVALRY
         Maurice Guiraud Riviere   b1881-
France.   c1925.   Silver.   18″ x 27″

         4591. WINDING YARN TIME
            By L. Grissard
         France.   c1925.   Silver.   Lady: 6″

4593. ILLUMINATION LADY
By P. Laurel
France.   c1930.   Gold.   Ht: 15″

4594. TWO BOUQUETS
By J.E. Cormier   (1869-1950)
France.   c1930.   Yellow.   Ht: 12½″

4595. COMING OF AGE
By Meier-Michel   b1880-
Austria.   c1925.   Black.   Ht: 16″

4596. NUDE WITH LIGHT
By Y. Guerbe
France.   c1925.   Green.   8″ x 14″
Glass lamp is signed "Daum".

4597. SCARF DANCE   by Denis
France.   c1935.   Green.   9½″
Quality white-metal casting.

1150

4598. FACETED STEPPER   Unsigned
    France.   c1930.   Yellow.   6″

4599. STEPPING OUT   by Leverrier
    Fr.   c1925.   Green.   6½″ Wh.-met.

4600. STAR DANCER   by D. Chiparus
    France.   c1920.   Pt: Yellow.   Ht: 20″

4602. PLEASANT PAUSE   by J. Daroles
    France.   c1933.   Black-brown.   11″ x 31″

4605. TURBANED BIRD GIRL
By A. Gory   Wk: c1895-1925
France.   c1920.   Pt: Silver.   Ht: 24"

4604. NUDE WITH HIGH BALL
By A. Gory   Wk: c1895-1925
France.   c1920.   Pt: Yellow.   Ht: 22"

4606. SITTING PRETTY   Unsigned
France.   c1928.   Pt: Gold.   Ht: 14"

4607. ON THE FENCE   Unsigned
France.   c1920.   Pt: Yellow, brown. c12"

4608. LITTLE MISS MUFFET
By Georges Rocher   Wk: c1895-1910
France.   c1905.   Pt: Yellow-brown.   10"   Seal #41.

4609. PRAYING GIRL   Unsigned
Fr.   c1920.   Pt: Brown/bisque.   Ht: 8"

4610. DUCK GIRL   Unsigned
Austria.   c1910.   Pt: Brown.   Ht: c6"

4606

4609

4607

4608

4610

4611. LE NID—The Nest
By Aristide Croisy
(1840-1899)
France. c1885. Brown. 6″
Original life-size marble completed
in 1882.

4612. IN THE PARK
By Nina Winkel
Amer. Dated: 1968. Red. 12″

4611

4612

4613. VICTORY
By Francois-Victor Cogné   (1870-1945)
France.   c1905.   Pt: Gold.   Ht: 33¼″   Seal #10
Fdr: Editeur Mottheau, Paris.
Inscription: *Alors La Marne Se Dressa!*

4614. NARCISSE
By Henri Léon Greber   b1855-
France.   c1903.   Pt: Gold doré.   26″, 35″, 46″
Fdr: Siot-Decauville, Paris.
Conserved: *Musée du Luxembourg.*

1154

4615

4616

4615. SEDUCTION OF DANAË—Greek Myth
    J. Emmanuel Descombs-Cormier   (1869-1950)
France.   c1928.   Pt: Gold-bronze.   Ht: 27″
Fdr: Susse Frères, Lost-wax, Paris.

Zeus, king of the gods, deflowers *Danaë* when he takes the form of a golden shaft of sunlight. He often used disguises to hide his amorous adventures from his wife Hera.

4616. LA NATURE SE DÉVOILANT—Unveiled
    Louis Ernest Barrias   (1841-1905)
France.   c1899.   Pt: Gold-bronze.   Ht: 27″
Fdr: Susse Frères, Lost-wax, Paris.

Original life-size version in tinted marble and Algerian Onyx in *Musée du Luxembourg*. First shown in Salon of 1899 and later displayed at Universal Exposition of 1900. *Mother Nature Disrobed* never became popular as his 1893 Salon entry, *La nature Mystérieuse et voilée se decouvre devant la Science.* See Volume II, #1387.

4617

4618

4619

4620

JEAN JACQUES PORRET
Swiss/American   Born 1941
See: Vol. II, Pages 454-455,
Vol. III, Pages 782-783

4617. METAMORPHOSES   by Jean Jacques Porret
America.   Dated: 10-1977.   Polished bronze.   Ht: 10″

4618. RECLINING   by Jacques Porret
America.   Dated: 1-1977.   Pt: Dark brown.   Ht: 17″

4619. NAPOLEON   by Jean Jacques Porret
America.   Dated: 8-1977.   Brown and bronze.   Ht: 19½″

4620. AMITY   by Jean Jacques Porret
America.   Dated: 1-1978.   Polished bronze.   Ht: 9″

4621. THE EMBRACE III   by Jean Jacques Porret
America.   Dated: 1-1977.   Pt: Dark brown.   Ht: 42½″

4622. RENCONTRE—Meeting   by J.J. Porret
America.   Dated: 6-1977.   Pt: Polished bronze, black.   40″

4623. MONUMENT—A Project   by J.J. Porret
America.   Dated: 5-1977.   Pt: Brown, Polished bronze.   23½″

4625. ONE HUNDRED PLEATS—Dancer
   By Démetre H. Chiparus   Wk: c1914-1933
France.   c1930.   Pt: Black, green, yellow.   14″
Black veined marble base,   5″.   Fdr: Etling.

4626. ODALISQUE—Turkish Harem Girl
   By Démetre H. Chiparus   Wk: c1914-1933
France.   c1933.   Pt: Yellow, gold, pink, green.
Ht: 15½″,   Green onyx: 4″. Also with round base.

4627. ILLUSION OF VIRTUE
   By Démetre H. Chiparus   Wk: c1914-1933
France.   c1925.   Pt: Silver, gold/ivory.   16″

4628. THE READER   White Metal/Ivorine
   By Menneville   Wk: c1920-1935
France.   c1925.   Black, silver.   Ht: c9 X 16″

Multi-colored base is marble and onyx veneer over
plaster. Menneville specialized in white metal
sculptures.

4629. SITTING PRETTY   White Metal/Ivorine
   By Menneville   Wk: c1920-1935
France.   c1930.   Pt: Green/ivorine.   Ht: 9"

4630. MUSICAL CLOCK   White Metal
   By Georges Lavroff   b1895-
France.   c1930.   Pt: Silver.   Ht: 16½" X 19½"

Lavroff attended the Beaux-Arts school in Moscow,
and later exhibited in the salons of Paris.

4631. LADY AND CAT by René Godard   b1886-
   France.   c1930.   Pt: Yellow.   Ht: c6"

Clock below not shown. Godard alternately signed
with two d's.

4632

4633

4634

4635

4636

4632-3. WIFE AND THE SHEIK   by Waagen
   Germany. c1900. Pt: Polychrome. 24¼" X 15"
High relief plaques are cast of a strong alloy
of white metals—very heavy.

4634. EASTERN WOMAN   by A. Gori or Gory
   France. c1910. Pt: Yellow. Ht: 29"   Base: 4"

4635. TAMBOURINE DANCER   Unsigned
   France. c1920. Pt: Brown/ivorine. Ht: c10"

4636. ARABIAN   by René Charles Massé   b1882-
   France. c1920. Pt: Dark brown. Ht: 13"

4638

4639

4640

4641

4638. LADY WITH HOUND
By Menneville   Wk: c1920-1935
France.   c1930.   Pt: Silver, black/ivorine.
Ht: 19''.   White metal.   Half-figure, shown to
left, has different head and dress design. The
rest of the sculpture is exactly the same.
Fdr: Rochard, Paris.

4639. AT THE BALL   by Faniose
Italy or France.   c1910.   Bronze/ivory.
Ht: 8''   Black, veined marble base: 1½''.

4640. THE MASKED BALL   White Metal
By Menneville   Wk: c1920-1935
France.   c1925.   Black, gold/ivorine.   17''

4641. THE DOVE   by Ignacio Gallo
Spain.   c1920.   Green, silver.
Hands, head of ivory.   Ht: 8''

4643. SALOME'S DANCE   by Henry Fugère
France. c1927.   Pt: Brown/ivory. 12"

This more expensive variation had a 3" contoured
octagonal base fitted with a beveled bronze underplate.
Ivory combination was available only in this size. Arm
bands cleverly conceal joints. Five hand carved ivory
sections and four separate bronze casts complete this
sculpture.

4642. ENCHANTRESS SALOME
    By Henry Fugère b1872-
France. c1927. Pt: Gold, black.   Ht: 12"
Gray and brown veined marble: 4"

The legs and top portion are fitted together
where number 4643 is ivory. Shown is middle
size of three editions cast in all bronze: 8½",
16".

4644. COMEDY-TRAGEDY DANCER
    By Joseph Descombs (1869-1950)
France. c1925. Pt: Gold/turquoise.
Three editions: 12¼", 16", 23"
Founder: Etling, Paris.

4645. MASK DANCER   by Joe Descombs
    France. c1925. Pt: Brown/ivory. 16"

Arms, legs and head are fitted into gown which is cast in
two pieces and joined at waist. Round bronze base is a
third casting.

4646

4647

4648

4646. BRISED AUTOMNE—Windy Autumn
By Maurice Bouval (1870-1920)
France. c1910. Pt: Yellow/ivory. Ht: 14″, *16″*
Ref: White bisque edition, Volume III, #1862.

4647. LISEUSE—The Reader
By Albert-Ernest Carrier-Belleuse (1824-1887)
France. c1895. Pt: Brown/ivory. Ht: 10″, 18″, 24″
Fdr: J. Chardon et Petit Fils, Paris. Active.
Ref: All bronze edition, Volume II, #1446.

4648. FILEUSE—The Spinner
By Albert-Ernest Carrier-Belleuse (1824-1887)
France. c1910. Pt: Gold tones/ivory. 28½″
Fdr: J. Chardon, Paris. Active. Three sizes.

4649. PANDORA by G. Flamand Wk: c1890-1925
France. c1920. Pt: Brown/alabaster. Ht: 10½″
Founder: H. Mazet, Paris.
Carved box is ivory, a gift from Zeus which Pandora should not
have opened—Greek myth. Gray marble base.

4649

4651.

4651.   LES AMIS DE TOUJOURS—Friends Forever
   By Démetre H. Chiparus   Wk: c1914-1933
France.   c1927.   Pt: Maroon, purple bodice, Gold
skirt/ivory. Ht: 11½″, 17″, 25″
Fdr: J. Chardon et Petit Fils, Paris.

Woman wears a *cloche* over her bobbed hair. Her
ivory hands rest on necks of two adoring Russian
borzois. Rectangular base is Brescia marble veneer
and carries signature of Chiparus. This very popular
and expensive work was cast over several years.
Condition and quality of ivory is best key to
determine approximate age.

4652. TIME TO REFLECT
   By A. Gori or Gory   Wk: c1895-1925
France.   c1910.   Pt: Gold doré/ivory.   Ht: 7"

Chair is hand carved, stained mahogany. Signed
on gown.

4653. KÖNIGLICH ADEL—Royal Aristocrats
   By Fritz Preiss and/or Otto Poertzel
Germany.   c1935.   Pt: Multi-color paint.   Ht: 18"
Founder: Preiss/Kassler, Monogram PK, Berlin.

Aristocrats was sold on this rectangular base, a
higher naturalistic base, and an octagonal three inch
bronze base with no marble. They are signed Preiss
or Poertzel. These two men worked together for a
time. Their signatures occasionally get switched—
probably due to the various presigned bases in the
foundry stock.

4657. EXOTIKORA
    Démetre H. Chiparus   Wk: c1914-1933
France.   c1920.   Pt: Black, brown/ivory.
Ht: 12″, *17″*, 24½″. Beige, brown bases.
Founder: Etling, Paris.

Dancer wears *cuirass* bodice with low
waistline in the manner of designer Léon
Bakst. Ivory inserts fill shoulder cut-outs.
Tonnelet skirt flares. Her toes curl in
slippers that match dress. Helmet design
copies the Ballet Russe *cloches*. Paris
was much influenced by the Russian
Ballet which was stranded there when
World War I broke out.

4656. KAPURTHALIAN DANSEUSE   by Démetre H. Chiparus
    France.   c1925.   Pt: Green and brown.   Ht: 16″
Ivory and bronze version offered in all three sizes.

4655. KAPURTHALIAN DANSEUSE—Punjab India
    By Démetre H. Chiparus   Wk: c1914-1933
France.   c1925.   Pt: Color varies/ivory.   Ht: 12″, *16″*, 22″
Offered on various shaped and colored marble bases.

4658. CÉRÉMONIEUX SYMÉTRIQUE
     By Démetre H. Chiparus
Fr.   c1925.   Pt: Brown/ivory.   15½″
Base is brown/white onyx.

4659. SHIELDA—Curtain Call
     By Démetre H. Chiparus   Wk: c1914-1933
France.   c1925.   Pt: Green, brown, red, silver/ivory.
Ht: *12″*, 18″. Base is brown Brescia, stratified marble.

Girl on tip-toes and wearing helmet has studded bodice.
Raised, pleated skirt forms a shield we interpret as a bow.

4660. Bayadère
     By Démetre H. Chiparus   Wk: c1914-1933
France.   c1924.   Pt: Brown, green, silver/ivory.   Ht: 15″   Base 5″

Triangular shaped base—when looking down—has signed bronze
plaque inset. Name *Bayadère* implies a dancing, singing entertainer of
southern India. It also describes the transversely striped and brightly
colored balloon shaped skirt. This interesting subject was edited with
same deluxe base in all bronze.

4661. **FELINES AWAKENING**
   By Démetre H. Chiparus   Wk: c1914-1933
France.   c1930.   Pt: Green, gold/ivory.   Ht: 13″
Cat emulating woman on plaque set in 6½″ base.

4662. **STARLIGHT DANCER**   by D.H. Chiparus
   France.   c1925.   Pt: Green pleated, handkerchief-
pointed hem skirt. Gold bodice has flaring cuffs and
matching helmet. Rectangular and curving, stratified-
marble base is shades of beige.   Ht: 13″, 22½″

4666. ASIAN DANCER   by Marcolin
    France.   c1930.   Pt: Gold, etc/ivory.   Ht: 12½''
Large, shallow green onyx base was ashtray.

4663. COSSACK DANCER   by D.H. Chiparus
    France.   c1924.   Pt: Brn/ivory.   Ht: 10½'', *17''*
Original marble base, 5'', is signed.

4664. TAMARA—After The Dance   by Chiparus
    Fr.   c1925.   Pt: Brn/ivory.   Ht: 6½'', *10'', 14½''*
Original, three tiered marble base is shown.

4667. THE TANGO
    By Démetre H. Chiparus   Wk: c1914-1933
France.   c1928.   Brown, black, gold/ivory. 24''

A Valentino type wears diamond patterned leotards
and a loose shirt. Lady has one piece dress
embroidered on top. Rectangular, stepped brown
marble base is signed.

4668. CON BRIO by Johann Philipp Preiss (1882-1943)
    Germany. c1930. Pt: Silver/ivory. Ht: 14½"
Tall layered, and low dish marble/onyx bases available.

4669. MOTH or ANT--Champagne Dancer by "Fritz" Preiss
    Germany. c1930. Pt: Green, silver/ivory. Ht: 17"
Shown on original brown onyx and black marble base.

4670. AUTUMN FASHION DANCER by "Fritz" Preiss
    Germany. 1927. Pt: Green, silver/ivory. Ht: 15"
On original green onyx and black marble base.

4672

4674

4671. TWO WAY--Dancer by F. Preiss
    Ger. c1925. Red, silver/ivory. 11"
Also offered with flowered skirt and cap.

4672. SPRING AWAKENING
    By "Fritz" Preiss (1882-1943)
Ger. c1935. Red, brown/ivory. 15"
Various colors of onyx and marble
were used in this single design.

4674. ANDREAN DANCER
    By Claire Colinet Wk: c1913-41
France. c1930. Gold/ivory. Ht: 11½"
Has S.P.A. monogrammed seal (coin).
These were sometimes initialed by the
artist Claire Jeanne Roberte Colinet.

4675

4676

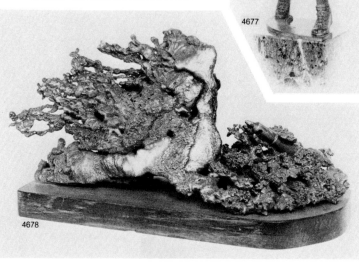

4678

4679

4677

MARIO SPAMPINATO Born 1915
Volumes: II,III, Pages: 456-7 & 769

Mario Spampinato, sculptor, founder (lost-wax process) and patineur, came to the United States from his native Italy and established an art workshop/foundry in 1956.

4675. SITTING GIRL—Nude Study 1972. Green tones. 13½"

4676. THE LADY GOLFER 1976. Pt: Light brown. Ht: 19"

4677. THE COMPLETED SERVE 1978. Pt: Light green. 21"

4678. ROCKET IN SPACE 1965. Grn/brn. & gold. 8" X 15"

4679. MARIO—Self Portrait 1976. Pt: Dark green. 20"

4680

4681

4682

4683

4684

4685

4686

4687

4688

COLLECTION FRANCAISE Seal #81

These small Art Nouveau, Art Deco and "assemblages" are cast from pure spelter (99.997% zinc), often called French bronze. Plastic "Ivorine" is employed to enhance some of the collection's works.

Selections on pages 1173-78, are contemporary casts from the 1900-1930 era original French molds. As such, they are known as "exemplaires"— not reproductions. The molds were acquired by J.B. Hirsch Company, in Brooklyn, New York from the original bankrupt founders.

Sculptural assemblages refer to rearrangements of mold sections to form new subjects. Notice the repeated use of some small figures on circus pages which are credited to J.E. Koster. Other works are by well known artists who rarely signed petite size editions like these. Two pieces, by D.H. Chiparus—most popular of the Decoists—are Danseuse #4697 and "Shielda" #4706 which is shown in the previous section.

4680. PIRATE Ht: 4"   4681. LA PIRATE Ht: 6½"
4682. GRANDE ECARTE by Van DeVoorde Ht: 13½" X 14"
4683. FILLE PICKWICK Ht: 4½"   4684. GARCON PICKWICK Ht: 4½"
4685. VIOLINISTE by D. Grisard c1925. Ht: 6"
4686. PAUVRE by Henry Fugére c1927. Ht: 6½"
4687. DANSEUSE DES INDES Ignacio Gallo c1925. Ht: 9" X 8"
4688. PIERRETTE by A. Lémo c1920. Ht: 9"
4689. JEUNE MARIEE by J. Ruel c1927. Ht: 8½"

4689

4690. CONTEMPLER H. Fugére c1927. 8"X 11"

4691. DANSE ESPECIALE by Van DeVoorde
    c1920. Ht: 12" X 11¼"

4692. SIRENE by Marcel Debut c1910

4693. CLEOPATRE by E. Movier
    c1922 Ht: 8½" 14"

4695. BALLERINE by Morante
    c1925. Ht: 10"

4696. DANSEUSE RAPIDE by E.Movier
    c1925. Ht: 8"

4697. DANSEUSE ARABE by D.H. Chiparus
    c1920. Ht: 6½"

4698. LA CHAUVRE-SOURIS Giraud-Rivière
    c1920. Ht: 6½"

4700

4701

4702

4703

4704

4705

4706

4707

4708

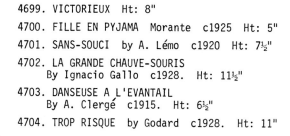

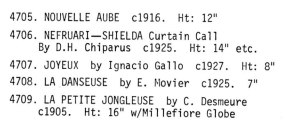

4709

4699. VICTORIEUX Ht: 8"

4700. FILLE EN PYJAMA Morante c1925 Ht: 5"

4701. SANS-SOUCI by A. Lémo c1920 Ht: 7½"

4702. LA GRANDE CHAUVE-SOURIS
    By Ignacio Gallo c1928. Ht: 11½"

4703. DANSEUSE A L'EVANTAIL
    By A. Clergé c1915. Ht: 6½"

4704. TROP RISQUE by Godard c1928. Ht: 11"

4705. NOUVELLE AUBE c1916. Ht: 12"

4706. NEFRUARI—SHIELDA Curtain Call
    By D.H. Chiparus c1925. Ht: 14" etc.

4707. JOYEUX by Ignacio Gallo c1927. Ht: 8"

4708. LA DANSEUSE by E. Movier c1925. 7"

4709. LA PETITE JONGLEUSE by C. Desmeure
    c1905. Ht: 16" w/Millefiore Globe

4710. CLOWN AUX BALLONS Koster Collage Ht: 7"
4711-12. LE FOU DE ROI 4½" CLOWN OBESE Ht: 4½"
4713. ACROBATIE Collage by J.E. Koster Ht: 5½"
4714. CLOWN A CHAVEL J.E. Koster Collage 10½"
4715. LES ACROBATES Assemblage Ht: 10"
4716-17. CLOWNS REVEUR Ht: 5½"
4718. JONGLEUR W/Millefiore Venetian Globe 12"
4719. PHOQUE JONGLANT J.E. Koster Collage 14½"
4720. LE PHOQUE—The Seal Ht: 5½"
4721. EN ROUTE POUR L'ECOLE Koster Collage 9"
4722. CHEVAL SCARED BY RABBIT Koster Collage
4723. PIERRETTE A L'OMBRELLE Koster Collage 8½"
4724. CLOWN A CERCEAU Ht: 5½"

4725. JEUNE FILLE Ht: 4½"

4726. DANTE by J. Ruel c1925. Ht: 7½"

4727-28. VIOLINCELLISTE et BEETHOVEN by Ruel
    c1925. Hts: 6½" and 5½"

4729. LE GRAND CHAPITEAU Assemblage J.E. Koster
    Ht: 20" X 12" Exciting circus scene.

4730

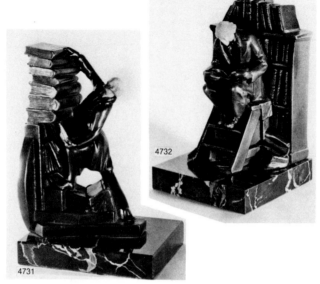

4732

4733

4734

4735

4736

4737

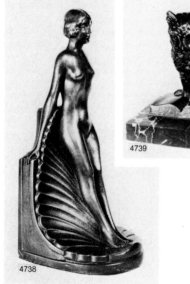

4738

4739

4740

4730. LE SINGE STUDIEUX Ht: 5½"

4731. SERRE LIVRES by Ruel c1925 7"

4732. BIBLIOTHECAIRE Ruel c1925 6½"

4733. LE SPHYNX Ht: 7¼"

4734. NEFERTITI DE EGYPTIENNE 3½"

4735. TETE DE CHEVAL Ht: 6"

4736. LE CHEVAL SAUVAGE Ht: 8"

4737. LE CHEVAL DE TROIE Ht: 7¼"

4738. ART DECO NU Guiraud-Rivière
      c1925. Ht: 9"

4739. LA CHOUETTE Ht: 5"

4740. LE LOUP Ht: 9½"

4741

HY LEVENS

Contemporary American sculptor, born in 1922, specializes in Western, sport and as shown here, biblical subjects. Much research plus great attention to detail is evident in all his works.

Italian founders were chosen to cast both "Daniel" and "David" in editions of thirty.

Series of his miniatures are presently displayed at the Hummelwerk showrooms.

Hy Levens is official sculptor/interpreter of Norman Rockwell limited editions.

4742. DAVID AND GOLIATH
     By Hy Levens b1922-
Italy. c1975. Dark brown. Ht: 17"
Marinelli Fdry., Florence, Italy.

4741. DANIEL IN THE LIONS' DEN
     By Hy Levens b1922-
Italy. c1978. Light brown. Ht: 15"
Venturi Arte Fdry., Bologna, Italy.

4742

4743

KABYLE AU RETOUR DE LA CHASSE
Paul Waagen (Sculp.)

4743. KABYLE AU RETOUR DE LA CHASSE by Waagen
France. c1880. Pt: Dark brown. Ht: 36"

Tunisian Berber tribesman, his dogs, and rescued lamb return
to the village in triumph with a predator's hide held aloft.
Reins shown are not original. Waagen specialized in Arabian
types and animals. Another Waagen did contemporary, turn of
the century (20th) people in sporting and beach attire. The
first names and details of their careers' remain a mystery.

4744

4745

4746

4747

4744. DERBY WINNER Pierre Jules Mêne (1810-1879)
      France. c1863. Pt: Brown. Ht: 9½'',16½'',
Number 16 in his catalogue. Considered to be one
of Mêne's finest compositions. Whip is missing.

4745. ERLN KOENIG Folk Ballad by Goethe c1811
      Attributed to Carl Kauba (1865-1922)
Austria. c1910. Pt: Brown. Ht: 7'' X 12''
Two tiered marble base 1½''. (The Elf King).

4746. DER ERLKÖNIG Goethe's Folk Ballad
      By George Hand Wright b1872-
Amer. Dated: 1916. Dark brown. Ht: 11''
Fdr: Griffoul, Newark, New Jersey.

4747. BARTOLOMMEO COLLEONE--Condottiere
      By Verrocchio (1435-1488)
Italy. c1900. Pt: Black. Ht: Reduction.
Monument cast by Alessandro Leopardi in 1492!

4748

4749

4750

CLEMENTE SPAMPINATO

Born in Italy, 1912, and studied at Rome and Paris academies before he settled in the United States. Presently a member of the National Sculpture Society, American Institute, Washington D.C., and the Gold Medal Artists' Committee.

He is ranked today as one of our leading "sports and Western" sculptors. His most renowned monument is the 12' Bobby Jones at the World Golf Hall of Fame.
Photos: Courtesy Campanile Galleries, Inc. Chicago, Illinois.

4748. BUFFALO HUNT 1954. Green. 18''
    Fdr: Modern Art Fdry., New York.

4749. THE GOLFER 1974. Brown. 30½''

4750. YOU CRAZY BAY 1973. Green. 27½''

4752. THE CHEYENNE
    By Carl Kauba (1865-1922)
Austria. c1905. Polychrome. Ht: 7'' X 11'

Carved natural granite base: 3''. Horse is
stamped Geschütz. Fine original casting
and hand painted patina.

4753. LOOKOUT John Massey Rhind (1860-1936)
    America. Dated: 1919. Brown. Ht: 21''
Founder: Roman Bronze Works, New York.

4754. PEACE PIPE Carl Kauba (1865-1922)
    America. c1978. Pt: Brown. Ht: 21''
Good quality contemporary cast. Marble: 2''

4755

4756

4757

4758

PONY EXPRESS

4759

4756. BRONCO BUSTER by Frederic Remington (1861-1909)
    Amer. 1978. Grey-brown. Ht: 17½'' Walnut base.
Original size 23'' cast by Roman Bronze Works, N.Y. and
sold by Tiffany & Co. This was F.R.'s first sculpture.
From authorized museum replica series by Remington.

4757. THE SIGNAL by Dell Weston Lost-Wax
    America. c1978. Pt: Brown. w/Walnut base: 8½''
Fdr: Dell Weston Fdry. Edition of fifty.

4755. INDIAN CHIEF by Bern-Schutt
    Amer. Dated: 1905. Dark brown. Diam: 8½''
Plaque cast for National Cash Register Co.

4758. THE DESPERADO by Carl Kauba (1865-1922)
    Austria. c1910. Pt: Polychrome. Ht: c24''
Horse and rider plunge from naturalistic base.

4760

4761

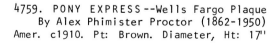
4762

4763

4759. PONY EXPRESS --Wells Fargo Plaque
By Alex Phimister Proctor (1862-1950)
Amer. c1910. Pt: Brown. Diameter, Ht: 17"

4760. RUNNING FIRE C. Kauba
Austria. c1910. Brown. 13" Rock: 2"
Surface imperfections on recent castings.

4761. LARIAT CHASE Carl Kauba
Austria. c1910. Polychrome. Ht: 11"
May be signed and/or stamped Geschutzt.

4762. LONE FEATHER G.M. Curtice
England/Amer. c1920. Pt: Brown.
Dimensions: 9½"X 7'. Stamped: GMC

4763. INDIAN CHARGE by A. Bofill
France. c1915. Pt: Gold/ivory.
Height: 16" Seal: #44.

4764. HUNTER'S TROPHY   Unsigned
    Austria. c1910. Pt: Brown. Ht: 9½"
Central section of fine inkwell set.

4765. NEST IN DANGER   Unsigned
    Austria. c1910. Red-brown. Ht: 11"
We attribute "Nest" and #4764 to Kauba.

4766. MOUNTAIN CLIMBER   Bruno Zack
    Germany. c1925. Yellow-gold. Ht: 6"

4767. THE COWBOY   by Edwin Bucher
    Swiss. c1920. Pt: Green/ivory. 14½"

4768. COWPUNCHER   by Carl Kauba
    Austria. c1915. Brown tones. Ht: 11"

4769. SOLDIER AT EASE
By Carl Kauba (1865-1922)
America. c1978. Pt: Brown tones.
Height: 18" Marble base: 2"

4771. THE WATER HOLE
An American Soldier
By Eugene Morahan b1869-
Amer. c1895. Dark brown. Ht: 20"
Fdr: Roman Bronze Works, N.Y.
Indian campaign of about 1880.

4772. STANDING SOLDIER Unsigned
Austria. c1920. Pt: Polychrome. Ht: 11½" w/rock.

4773. EXHAUSTED SOLDIER by Hans Müller b1873-
Austria. c1920. Pt: Gray-black. Ht: 7"

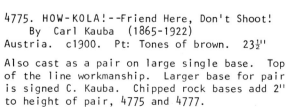

4775. HOW-KOLA!--Friend Here, Don't Shoot!
    By Carl Kauba (1865-1922)
Austria. c1900. Pt: Tones of brown. 23½"

Also cast as a pair on large single base. Top
of the line workmanship. Larger base for pair
is signed C. Kauba. Chipped rock bases add 2"
to height of pair, 4775 and 4777.

4778. ARAB CHIEFTAINS   Unsigned
    Austria. c1900. Polychrome. Ht: 14½"
White naturalistic granite/quartz bases.
Fdr: Franz Bergman, Vienna. Seal #77

Pair is probably by Kauba. His style and
proportions are quite evident. These are
among the finest pair of Vienna bronzes we
have seen. Artist painted patinas.

4778

4779

4779. ARAB MARAUDER
By Jean Baptiste Belloc
Worked: c1889-1914
France. c1900. Pt: Brown tones.
Ht: 22" Seal #19. Fdr: R. Cottin.

Arab chief, on wounded camel (arrow
through hind leg) holds female head
aloft as he rides for camp with his
abducted maiden strapped to saddle.
She holds dagger poised, readied to
kill herself rather than be used at
her captor's pleasure. Work is one
of Belloc's exciting, morbid action
creations--his most popular.

4781. DANGEROUS LOVE Unsigned Fr. c1900. Ylo-brn. 12"

4782. CONQUEST by Johann-Baptist Schreiner born: 1866-
      Germany. c1900. Pt: Dark brown. Ht: 9½"

4783. SUMMIT Charles Lemoine born: 1839-
      France. c1870. Pt: Black, gold. Height: 28"

4784. YOUNG FALCONER Ernst Gustav Jaeger born: 1880-
      Berlin. c1910. Brown. c12" Fdr: Lauchammer Bild.

4785. VENUS--Vatican marble Daedalus c400AD
      France. c1900. Brown. Fdr: Barb. 7,10½,14,26½,35"

4786. MARATHON SOLDAT--Louvre J.P. Cortot (1787-1843)
      Fr. Marble: 1833. Bronze: c1890. 15,20,26,38½" Seal #6

4787. TORCH H. Keck Ger. c1910. Yellow-brown. 11"

4788. FAMILY SEAL Unsigned. Amer. c1920. Brown. Ht: 5"

4789. LION TAMER Unsigned Aust. c1890. Grn-brn. 6½"

4790. BIRD HUNTER Unsigned Austria. c1890. Dark brown. Ht: 7"

4791. RABBIT HUNTER Füllborn Ger. c1915. Green-brown. Ht: 7"

4792. HIKER A. Brest Holland. c1910. Pt: Gray-black. Ht: 8½"

4793. CHASSEUR Ferville-Suan Fr. c1885. Brown. 7½" Med. au Salon.

4794. TAM O' SHANTER Fdr: Gladenbeck Ger. c1900. Pt: Brown. Ht: 11½"

4795. SOTZWNÖLFÜZPHLOYU--All's Well by Karl Hackstock (1855-1919)
    Austria. c1890. Pt: Dark brown and green. Ht: 13½"

4796. LASZLOMIKLOS by Mihaly Telcs born: 1872-
    Budapest, Hungary. c1905. Pt: Brown-green. Ht: 19"

4797. TOM THUMB by Mihaly Telcs--Medal 1900 Universal Exposition
    Budapest, Hungary. 1898. Pt: Dark brown-black. Ht: 15½"

4798

4799

4801

4802

4803

4800

4804

4805

4806

AUSTRIAN/VIENNA
BRONZES
c1900-c1920

These small sculptures are hand
painted by foundry artists who
paid great attention to detail.
Only one foundry is presently
active in Vienna and their production is still of high quality
but very limited. Ref: Volume
III, pages 758-763.

4810

4811

4807

4808

4809

4812

4813

4814

4815

4798. ARAB SCRIBE   Ht: 3"

4799. HOT DRINKS   Ht: 3"

4800. SLAVE AUCTION   Ht: 12"

4801. OSTRICH GROUP   Ht: 14"

4802. ARMS DEALER   Ht: 4½"

4803. VASE PAINTER   Ht: 5½"

4804. PEACOCK FEATHERS   Ht: 11½"

4805. MOSLEM PRAYER   Ht: 5¼"

4806. JEWELRY MERCHANT   Ht: 7"

4807. MOUNTED FALCONER   Ht: 9"

4808. DESERT CROSSING   Ht: c12"

4809. MEDITATION   Ht: c5"

4810. SLAVE AUCTION   Ht: 5"

4811. SNAKE CHARMER   Ht: 2"

4812. MOROCCAN SOLDIER   Ht: 5½"

4813. ARAB SOLDIER   Ht: 10"

4814. ARAB RIFLEMAN   Ht: c10"

4815. SNAKE CHARMER   Ht: 17" Wh-met.

4819

4816

4817

4818

4820

4821

4822

4816. PETIT TAMBOUR STHRAU
     By Léon Fagel (1851-1913)
France. Salon: 1905. Pt: Brown.
Three editions cast of "Drum-
mer of Wattignies" Monument Was
unveiled at Avesnes, Sept. 1905.

4817. HESSIAN by G. Massa
     Roma. c1890. Brown. 15½"
Bayonet percussion rifle, c1830.

4818. VIELLE GARDE
     Armond Jules LeVéel 1821-1905
Fr. c1880. Brown. 15" Fdr: Susse

4819. OLD GUARD by Schrodel
     Fr. c1890. Brown/ivory. 6"

4820. SCOT SOLDIER Unsigned
     Fr. c1900. Red-brown. 5"

4821. TAMBOUR by Duhousset
     Fr. c1900. Pt: Black. 10½"

4822. QUAND VOUS VOUDREZ
     By C. Anfrie born: 1886-
Fr. c1910. Pt: Gold. Ht: 24"
Salon Des Beaux Arts--Heros
of Alsace-Lorrain.

4824. EN GUERRE--At War
    By Mathurin Moreau (1822-1912)
France. c1900. Pt: Red-brown. Ht: 23"
Hors Concours, Fdr: Bisset, Paris.
Young French foot soldier wears full pack and
war weary expression. Mathurin Moreau is best
known for his lighter themes though he did some
excellent patriotic monuments as seen here.

4826. AVANT LE COMBAT--Volontaire de 1792
    By Etienne-Henri Dumaige (1830-1888)
France. c1872. Pt: Dark brown. Ht: 25½"
Executed Hors Concours--out of competition.
Reference: "Après Le Combat", Vol. II, #1506.

4828. QUAND MÊME
    By Antonin Mercié (1845-1916)
France. Dated: 1883. Pt: Brown. Ht: 34"
Fdr: Barbedienne, Paris. Seal #6 Con't.

4828. Three other editions by Barbedienne were
25", 43", and 50"—from 1906 catalogue.
Equally popular to "Gloria Victis" is Mercié's
"Quand Même" executed for the city of Belfort,
1882, of which a copy stands on the site of the
former Palais des Tuileries.

An Alsacian mother seizes the musket falling from
the hands of her wounded son and stands on the de-
fense against the Germanic foe. This subject is
very dramatic, pathetic and it is skillfully kept
within bounds by the sculptor.

4831. L'ARMÉE by A.O. Croisy (1840-1899)
    France. c1871. Dark brown. Ht: 25½" etc.
Founder: Susse Fréres, Paris et Arcueil, France.

4832

4832. L'INVASION—Monument in miniature
   By Onésyme-Aristide Croisy (1840-1899)
France. c1873. Brown tones. 24" Susse Fréres.

Croisy became very popular during and after the Alsace-Lorraine
conflict, 1870-1. Among his triumphs were "The Invasion" for the
city of Orleans and exhibited in Salon of 1873; "The Army" of the
Loire, done in 1871 and exhibited in the Salon of 1885; Monument
commemorating the "Sons of Ardennes", 1895; and "Guerre de 1870"
unveiled at Villars-Fontaine, 1896. These are but a few of his
works listed in Dictionnaire des Sculpteurs by S. Lami, 1914.

4834. REGIMENT D'INFANTRIE
    By C. Anfrie Wk: c1880-1915
France. c1899. Pt: Brown tones. Ht: 26", 33"
Soldier guards 113th Infantry banner. Note pistol.

4835. MARINE BUGLER
    By C. Anfrie Wk: c1880-1915
France. c1890. Pt: Dark brown. Ht: 9½", 16"

4836. RESTAFETTE—Survivor War 1871
    By C. Anfrie Wk: c1880-1915
France. Dated: 1888. Pt: Brown, green. Ht: 24"
Salon of Beaux Arts, 1888 commemorating the famous
33rd Dragoon of Franco-Prussian War.

4838. CALL TO ARMS
 By Paul-Francois Choppin b1856
France. c1886. Pt: Brown. Ht: c18",35"
Represents an American Revolutionary Patriot
of 1775. See "Minute Man" of D. Chester French
in Volume III, #2633.

4840. TEDDY ROOSEVELT—As a Rough Rider
 By Joahnnes-Sophus Gelert b1852-
America. c1897. Pt: Gray-brown. Ht: 20½"
Gelert was born in Denmark, studied in Italy
and exhibited in the United States and France.
Founder is Mauser Mfg. Co., Philadelphia.

4841

4842

4843

4844

4845

GRENADIER 1916

1200

4848

4849

4846

4847

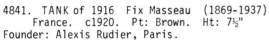

4850

4851

4841. TANK of 1916 Fix Masseau (1869-1937)
France. c1920. Pt: Brown. Ht: 7½"
Founder: Alexis Rudier, Paris.

4842. ARMORED CAR of 1916 by A. Cuvek
France. c1920. Pt: Brown, silver. 3½"

4843. RALLY-HO by D. Grissard
France. c1885. Pt: Brown tones. 33½"

4844. LA GARDE MEURT ETNE SE REND PAS
By Lord Ronald S. Gower died-1915
France. c1885. Pt: Gold paint. 15" X 19½"

4845. GRENADIER—1915
By G. Flammand Wk: c1890-1925
France. c1920. Pt: Dark brown. Ht: 12¼"

4846. NAPOLEON Eugène Marioton (1854-1925)
France. c1890. Brown. Ht: 15", 26½"

4847. THE ARTS by Waagen White-metal
France. c1890. Pt: Brown. Ht: 24½"

4848. ADOLF HITLER Franz Seifert b1866-
Germany. c1935. Yellow. Ht: 6¼"

4849. F. ROOSEVELT Jo Davidson (1883-1952)
America. Dated: 1934. Pt: Brown. Ht: 5"
Founder: A.C. Rehberger & Co., Chicago.

4850. ATTAQUE Théophile Somme b1871-
France. c1910. Pt: Brown tones. Ht: c10"

4851. AWAITING HIS OPPONENT
By Godefroid de Vreese b1861-
Belgium. Dated: 1898. Pt: Dark brown. Ht: 15"
Son of Constant and student of Simonis and Van der
Stappen, Brussels. He also did medals and is repre-
sented in several museums.

4852

4853

4854

4855

4856

4857

4858

4852. POWERFUL YOUTH—Bust by J. Gossin
France. c1880. Brown. Hts: 10", 15"

4853. GRECIAN BUST   Barbedienne Seal #6
France. c1900. Dark brown. 6" etc.

4854. KING ALBERT OF BELGIUM (1909-34)
By Mary Winfield Mason
America. Dated: 1915. Dark brown. Ht: 9"

4855. JEUNE GUERRIER—Young Warrior
By Emmanuel Hannaux b1855-
France. c1895. Brown. 6½", 9", 21½", 31"
Fdr: Colin, Paris. Med. d'Honneur.

4856. ABRAHAM LINCOLN—Half Figure
By George Grey Barnard b1863-
America c1910. Pt: Brown. Ht: 28½"
Represented in Metropolitan Museum, N.Y.

4857. MENSCH ZEITGENÖSSISCH
By Wilhelm Haverkamp b1864-
Ger. Dated: 1898. Brown. Ht: 21½" etc.
Fdr: Friedrichshagen, Berlin.

4858. MAN   Raffaelo Romanelli 1856-1928
      Italy. c1900. Pt: Brown. Ht: 25"

4859. ROYALTY by Ernest Rancoulet
      France. c1900. Brown-yellow 27½"

4860. BATTLE SCENE   Emile Pinedo
      France. c1890. Gold doré. Ht: 6"

4861. EAST-WEST BATTLE   Unsigned
      France. c1860. Green-brown. 12½"

4862. L'EMIR—Persian Officer Unsigned
      France. c1875. Silver. 29" Wh-met.

4864. ANDRE MAIRE de LILLE 1792—French Patriot
By Jules Dechin (1869-1941)
France. Dated: 1907. Pt: Dark brown. Ht: 21½"
Fdr: Bingen et Costenoble, Paris. Active: 1880-

4865. MIRABEAU—1749-1791
By André F. Truphème (1820-1888)
France. Dated: 1857. Pt: Brown. 18" etc.
Fdr: E. Colin & Cie., Paris.
French lover, politician, revolutionary
leader and orator.

4866. MOLIÈRE—1622-1673 Satirist
Etienne M. Mélingue (1808-1875)
France. c1850. Brown. 18" Fdr: Susse

4867. CIMABUE—The Painter
Pierre E. Delpech
France. Dated: 1873. Gray-black. 19"

4868. EUGENE DELACROIX—1887
Aime-Jules Dalou (1838-1902)
France. c1889. Dark brown. Ht: 8"
Fdr: A.A. Hebrard—sizes to 35"

4866. MOLIÈRE. Mélingue

4867. (base inscription unclear)

4868.

4869. BONAPARTE—Médaillon in Louvre
By David d'Angers (1788-1856)
France. Dated: 1832. Green-brown. 6"

4870. RICHARDSON, Samuel—British Novelist
England. c1882. Pt: Dark brown. Ht: 8½"
Miniaturized monument of Richardson, 1689-1887.

4871. SHAKESPEARE—1564-1616 by A. Carrier (1824-1887.
France. c1875. Pt: Tones of brown. Hts: 22" etc.

4873

4872

4874

4875

4872. GÄNSEMÄNNCHEN—Geeseman
    By Pancraz Labenwolf (1492-1563)
Germany. c1900. Pt: Yellow-brown. Ht: 6"

Miniatures of this well known sixteenth-century
fountain in Nurnberg, Germany have been cast in
many editions of bronze, white metal, etc., and
still is a popular subject for wood carvers.

4873. DER HÜHNER DIEB—The Chicken Thief
    By Hermann Joachim Pagels b1876-
Germany. Dated: 1910. Dark brown. Ht: 12"
Set on 11" sloping octagonal wood base. This
is one of several bronze reductions of popular
fountain at Aachen, Germany.

4874. RINGEN DER NACKEN by Elischer
    Austria. Dated: 1920. Brown-green. 7½"
Black/white marble base, 2" Ref: Vol. II, #1175
Elischer was master of the tense moment.

4875. POTAGE À LA POUSSIN—Chicken Soup
    By Lalouette
France. c1900. Pt: Yellow-brown. Ht: 13"
Mottled, red marble base w/underplate, 1½"

PART TWO
References

4876

4876. ANNALAMP White-metal
France. c1925. Polychrome Ht: 22"
Fine, high-style Deco figure was mounted
on marble veneer clock. Soft illumination
came from one of several choices of globes.

Founders' Seals

81

82A

82

83

84

85

86

87

88

89

90

91

Volume I #01 through #24
Volume II #01 through #58
Volume III #59 through #80
Volume IV #81 through #91

SCULPTORS
Keyed to the Photographic Section

-A-
ABRAHAM, R.   3338
AGASIAS   3443
AICHELE, P.   3996 4208 4316 4317
             4345
d'AIRE, P.   3992
AITKIN, R.I. 3708
AIZELIN, E.A.   4460 4469 4484
ALAPHILIPPE, C.   4076
ALLEGRAIN, C-G.   4223
ALLIOT, L.   3922
ALONZO, D.   3842 3849 3985 3989
             3991
ANDRE, A.   3875
ANDREAS   3324 4229
ANDREE, P.   3497 4392
ANFRIE, C.   3191 3192 3211 3664
             3665 3667 3815 4053
             4822 4483 4834 4835
             4836
ANGLES, J.   3795
ANIE-MOUROUX, Mme.   3809
ASTORI, E.   3680
AUBAN, P.C.   3734
AUBE, J-P.   4089
AUBERT, J-A. 3655 3656
        -B-
BANDINELLI, B.   4136
BARBEDIENNE, F.   4066 4853
BARBELLA, C. 3690
BARILLOT, E. 4328
BARNARD, G.G.   4856
BARNER   4014 4437
BARRIAS, L.E.   3487 4378 4532
             4616
BARTH, W.   3917
BARTHOLEME, A.   4106
BARYE, ALF.   4152
BARYE, ANT.   4155
BASTIAN, O.   3243
BAUBIEN   3874
BAYER-SCHULTE, H. 3223
BECK, E.   3240 3290 3291 3337
             3399 3481
BELLOC, J.B. 4779
BENDA, B.   3237
BENELAIRE   4477
BENK, J.   4275
BERCHMANS, O.   390A
BERGMAN, F.   3584 3586 3596 3600
BERN-SCHUTT   4755
BERNAUER, F. 4156
BERNEVITZ   3921
BERNOUD, E.   3844
BERTHIER, P. 3832

BETLEN, G.   3863
BEZNER, M.   4364
BISCHOFF, A. 3512
BITTER, A.J-L.   4585
BLACZ   4004
BLANCHON, M. 3457
BOFILL, A.   3305 3485 3918 4474
             4521 4763
BOIZOT, L.S. 4150
BOLDARIN   4170
BOLOGNA, G.   3461 4133
BONHEUR, I.   3368 4545 4550
BORANE   3435
BOSIO, B.   3721
BOUCHER, A.   3281 4391
BOUCHER, J.   3352
BOULLOT, R.   3205 3206
BOURAINE, M. 3724 4016
BOURET, E.   3199 321B 3730 4414
BOUVAL, M.   3920 4646
BOYD, M-S.   4251
BRAHN, G.M.   4137
BRANDEL, A.   4371
BRANDT, F.   3235 3236
BREST, A.   4792
BRONIER, A.   3311 3312
BROOKS, H.   3712
BROSE, R.C.   4312
BRUCHON, E.   3182 3183 3489
BUCHER, E.   4767
BUGLER, V.   3424
BUHOT, L-C.H.   4443
BURROUGHS, E.W.   326B
        -C-
CAIN, A-N.   3878 4081 4369
CAMPAGNE, P-E.D. 4285
CANOVA, A.   3436 3448
CALMELS, C.   3961
CARDONA, J.   4290
CARLIER, E.N.   4074 4523
CARPEAUX, J.B.   3908
CARRIER BELLEUSE, A.E. 3524 3662
             3663 3735 4083 4113
             4154 4180 4346 4447
             4456 4647 4648 4871
CARTINET   4258 4259 4276
CASINI, E.   3484
CAUSSE, J.   3803 3900 3945 4301
             4479
CECIONE, A.   4093
CERIBELLA, C.   4051
CERNIGLIANI-MELILLI   3834 3870
CHALON, L.   3851 3855
CHAPU, H.M.A.   3915 4495

SCULPTORS

CHARPENTIER, F-M.   3654 3929
CHAUDET, A-D. 4048
CHENIER   4386
CHEURET, A.   4472 4473
CHILMEAU, G. 3635
CHINROZZI   4539
CHIPARUS, D.H.   3682 3738
                     3739 3954 3997
                     3998 3999 4000
                     4024 4110 4600
                     4625 4626 4627
                     4651 4655 4656
                     4657 4658 4659
                     4660 4661 4662
                     4663 4664 4667
                     4697 4706
CHOPPIN, P.F. 4838
CHOTKA   3614
CHRETIEN, E-E.   3273
CHRISTOFLE   4528 4529
CHRISTOFORO-VICARI 3843
CLARA, J.   3683 3686
CLEMENCIN, A.F.   3301
CLERGE, A.   4703
CLERGET, A. 3750 3751
CLESINGER, J-B.   4179
CLODION, C.M. 392A 4085 4166
                     4167 4169 4175
                     4176 4177 4178
                     4181
COCHERET, L. 4132
COGNE, F-V. 4613
COLINET, C.J.R.   3347 4228
                     4267 4674
COLOMBO, A. 3820
COLOMBO-GRANG 4050
CONSTANT-ROUX 3444 3445
CONSTANT, M. 3287 3292 3344
CONSTANT, Y. 3833
CORMIER, J.E. 4594
CORTOT, J.P. 4786
COUDRAY, F.G. 3638
COUDRAY, G.C. 3804 3827 3828
                     4344 4424
COUTAN, J-F. 400A
CROISY, O.A. 4611 4831 4832
CURTICE, G.M. 4762
CUVEK, A.   4842
              -D-
DAEDALUS   4785
DAILLION, H. 4219
DAMMANN, P.M. 4576
DAMBOISE, M. 4065
DAROLES, J. 4602
D'ASTE, J.   3691 3692 3694
             4115

DAUVERGNE, J.   4230
DAVID d'ANGERS   4356 4869
DAVIDSON, J. 4849
DEBUT, J-D. 3995 4467
DEBUT, M.   3637 3866 3935
             4045 4692
DECHIN, J.   4864
DEIHLE, G.   3231
DELAGRANGE, L-N. 3807 3858
DELANNOY, M. 4250 4573
DELAPLANCHE, E.   4353 4415
DELIN, K.   3376
DELPECH, P.E. 4867
DENIS   4597
DERCHEU, J-A-A.   4240
DESBOIS, J. 3682
DESCOMPS, J.E.   3576 3577
                  3939 3980 4023
                  4594 4615 4644
                  4645
DESLONGCHAMPS, L. 4471
DESMEURE, C. 3169 3170 4709
DETRIER, P-L 3531 3532
DeVOORDE, VAN 4682 4691
DeVRIEZ   3982
DIGONATA, M. 3825
DORIOT   3161
DOUAY, M-C. 4362
DRAH (HARDL) 3896 4151
DROUOT, E.   3318 3495 3533
             3534 3634 3905
             4054 4070 4341
             4379 4410 4520
             4524 4525
DUBUCAND FILS, A.E.   3522
DUHOUSSET   4821
DUMAIGE, E-H. 3294 3493 4461
             4462 4463 4826
DUMAINE, E.H. 4098
DUMANGE, G. 4026
DUPLAN et SALLES 4031 4032
DURET, F.J. 4299
              -E-
EBERLEIN, G.H.   4252
EHLEDERSOHNE, M. 4307
EICHHORN, G. 4073
EICHLER, K   4207
EISENBERGER, L.   3387 3389
                  3396 4216 4506
ELISCHER   4874
ETCHETO, J. 3315
              -F-
FAGEL, L.   4816
FALCONET, E-M.   4225
FANIOSE   4639
FAURE de BROUSSE V.D. 4384

FAYRAL 4589	GRAEFNER, L. 3471
FELDERHOFF, R. 4196	GRATCHEFF, I. 3545 3548
FERNAND 3736	GREBER, H.L. 4614
FERVILLE-SUAN 4793	GREGOIRE, J-L. 3728 4069
FERY 3885	4162 4164
FESSLER, L. 4350	GREVIN, A. 4390
FLAMAND FLAMMAND, G. 3933	GREIER, E. 3266
3949 4649 4845	GRISARD, D. 4685 4843
FLAMEN, A 4135	GRISSARD, L. 4591
FORETAY, A-J. 3835 4418	GRUBER 3906
FRANK, M. 3391	GUERBE, Y. 4596
FREMIET, E. 3349 3361 4160	GUERY, P-J. 3710
FRICK, F. 336A	GUEYLOS, G. 4318
FRISHMUTH, H.W. 4244 4247	GUILLAUME, E-O. 4355
FUGERE, H. 4642 4643 4686	GUILLEMIN, A. 3518
4690	GUILLEMIN, E. 4314 4315
FULLBORN 3229 3333 3381	GUIRAUD-RIVIERE, M. 4206
4791	4238 4590 4698
FUNK, V. 3258	4738
-G-	GURADZE, C.H. 3543
GALLO, I. 4641 4687 4702	GURBE, R. 4574
4704	GURSCHNER, G. 3868 3907
GAMBOGE 3238	GYCON 4149
GARBAND 4078	-H-
GARNIER, J. 3222 3606 3793	HAASE-ILSENBURG, H. 3375
3794 3913	4556 4559
GASQ, P. 4481	HACKSTOCK, K. 4300 4795
GASS, F. 3275	HAFFENRICHTER, H. 3511
GAUDEZ, A-E. 3165 3176 3177	HALOU, A.J.B. 4533 4534
3274 3309 3490	HAMBURGER, E. 3426 3427
3648 4420 4440	4338
4445 4485 4498	HANNAUX, E. 4855
GAUQUIE, H.D. 4096	HANNES, A. 3678
GAUTHERIN, J. 4529	HARDL II, M. 4151
GEIER, E. 4329	HARTWELL, C.L. 4572
GELERT, J.S. 4840	HARTZER, F. 4575
GERMAIN, J.B. 3932 4422 4426	HASE 3897
4487	HAVERKAMP, W. 4857
GERMAINE-OURG 4547	HEBERT, P-E. 4034 4090 4186
GILBERT, A. 4010 4581	HEINEMANN, F. 3421
GIRARDON, F. 4134	HENIES, H. 3219
GIRAUD, H. 4486	HERING, W. 3892
GLUMER, H.W. VON 4541	HERTEL, O. 3373
GLYCON 4149	HIBBARD, F.C. 3631
GODARD, A. 4103 4704	HIOLIN, L-A. 3638 4373
GODARD, R. 4631	HOFER-CASSEL 4319
GODET, H. 3802	HOFER-CREFELD 4270 4319
GORNIK, F. 3547	HOFFMAN, O. 4538
GORY/GORI, A. 3588 3847 3848	HOFFMANN 3326
3958 3984 3987	HOFFMANN, H. 3434
3990 4604 4605	HOLAND, C. 3335
4634 4652	HOLLWECK, L. 4273
GOSSIN, J. 4852	HOTTET, L. 3207 3208 4087
GOTZ, J. 3475	HOVE, V. VAN 3650
GOTZE/GOETZ, M. 3262 3263	HUBERT, R. 3244
3265 4334	HUMPLIK, J. 367B
GOWER, R.S. 4492 4844	HUSSMAN, A. 4554

SCULPTORS

HUZEL 3449 353A

-I-

IFFLAND, F. 3210 3398 3401
3659 4127 4128
4130 4295 4302
4321 4505

-J-

JACOBS, H. 3829
JAGER/JAEGER, G. 3277 3329
3394 4226
JAEGER, E.G. 4227 4784
JAEGER, R. 4234
JAHN, A. 3640 3641 4502
JANENSCH, G.A. 3247 3250
4357
JAQUET, D-A. 331A
JARAY, S. 3978
JENSEN, F. 3285
JENSEN, P.M. 3367 3380 3397
3468
JOBLINGER 3303
JOLA, J. 3857
JONCHERY, C. 3977 4057
JOSSELIN 3886
JOUST, A. 4503
JUST, A. 4280 4323
JYPAGNE, W. 3542

-K-

KAESBACH, R. 3218 4187 4246
4342 4580
KAHILL, V. 3702
KALISH, M. 4296
KANN, L. 3883
KAUBA, C. 3568 3672 4056
4063 4064 4561
4562 4563 4564
4565 4566 4567
4745 4752 4754
4758 4760 4761
4765 4768 4769
4775 4777 4778
KAUFMANN, H. 3221
KECK, H. 3418 3472 3520
3676 4236 4278
4787
KELETY, A. 3957 4055
KERVERSEAU, G. de 4239
KEYSER, E.W. 3877
KICHUT 3384
KISSNER, A. 3246
KLEY, L. 4322
KOCA, J. 4707
KOLBE, G. 4218
KORBEL, M. 3703
KORN, J-R. 4548
KORSCHAN, C. 3864 3881 3882
3923
KOSSOWSKI Jr., H. 4052

KOSTER, J.E. 4710 4713 4714
4719 4721 4723
4729
KOWALCZEWSKI, K. 3300 3517
3810 3811 3956
4060 4071 4220
4376 4516
KOWALCZEWSKI, P.L. 3228 3267
3413 4209 4217
4434 4509 4510
4519
KREMEN, V.N. 3558
KRIPPEL, H. 3623
KRUSE, C.M. 3456 4121 4122
4123
KUCHLER, R. 3364 3473 3474
3507 351B 4311

-L-

LABENWOLF, P. 4872
LABROUE, E. de 4168
LALOUETTE 3644 4875
LAMY, E.L. 3313
LANCERAY, I.A. 3550 3551
3552 3553 3554
3556 3560
LANGE, R.W. 3249 3509
LANYI 4537
LAPORTE, E. 4067 4385
LaPORTE, E-H. 3503
LARCHE, R. 3340 4404 4408
4409
LATT, H. 3679
LAUREL, P. 4593
LAURENT, E. 3817 3818 4497
LAVAYSSE, A. 4582
LAVERGNE, A-J. 3319 3320
LAVROFF, G. 4630
LeBROC, J.B. 4068
LECOURTIER, P. 4368
LEDERMANN 3440
LEDRU, A. 3860 3919
LeFAGUAYS, P. 4268 4269 4587
LeFEUVRE, L.A. 3701 4544
LEFEVRE-DESLONGCHAMPS 4471
LeFEVRE, C. 3733
LEIBKUCHLER, P. 3438 3455
4198
LEJEUNE 4265
LEMO, A. 4688 4701
LEMOINE, C. 4783
LEOCHARES 3447
LEOPARDI, A. 4747
LEONARD, A. 3605 3607
LEPKE/LEPCKE, F. 3519 4351
4399
LERCHE, H. St. 3909
LEROUX, F.E. 3209
LEROUX, G. 4030

LESUEUE	3872		
LETTON	4320		
LEVASSEUR, H.L.	3261	3269	
	3271	3428	4199
LeVEEL, A.J.	4818		
LEVENS, H.	4741	4742	
LEVERRIER	4589	4599	
LEVISSEUR	3195	3196	
LIBERICH, N.	3555		
LIEBMANN, H.	4213		
LINDENBERG, M.	3666		
LIPSCHYTZ, S.	4022		
LOEBE, A.	3422		
LOEWENTHAL, A.I.	4243		
LOISEAU-BAILLY, G.	4013		
LOISEAU-ROUSSEAU, P.	3801		
LORENZL, J.	4264	4266	4306
LOUCHET, C.	3756	3757	3925
	3931		
LUDOVISI, B.	3430		
LUGERTH, F.	3390	4009	4044

-M-

MADRASSI, L.	3321	3446	3831
	4084	4446	4448
MAINDRON, H.	4530		
MALAVOLTI, H.	3660		
MANIN	3837		
MANTURE	4416		
MANZ, E.	3506		
MANZOLLO, A.	4288		
MARCELLIN, J-E	3719		
MARCH, S.	3483		
MARCOLIN	4666		
MARCUSE, R.	333A	3420	
MARIE, D-P-L.	4395		
MARIOTON, C	4407		
MARIOTON, E.	3288	3796	4361
	4412	4846	
MARSY II, G.	4135		
MARULKA	3704		
MASON, M.W.	4854		
MASSA, G.	4817		
MASSE, R.C.	4636		
MASSEAU, F.	4841		
MASTON, A.	4025		
MATETA, J.	3622		
MATHET, L.	4037		
MAUSKE, P.	4557		
MEDNAT	4061	4111	
MEIER, K.L.	4256		
MEIER-MICHEL	4595		
MELINUE, E.M.	4866		
MELOLLE	3164		
MENE, J.P.	4744		
MENNEVILLE	4628	4629	4638
	4640		
MERCIE, A.	3451	4828	

MEUNIER, C.	3268		
MICHAEL-ANGELO	3429		
MICHEL, G.F.	4403		
MICHEL-PASCAL, F.	4356		
MIRVAL, C.	3698		
MOBIUS, K.	3403		
MOIGNIEZ, J.	4545		
MOLITOR, M.	3395		
MONCEL de PERRIN, A.	4514		
MONGINOT, C.	4104		
MONTAGNE, M.	3459		
MORAHAN, E.	4771		
MORAILE	3674		
MORANTE	4695	4700	
MOREAU, A.	3166	3173	3173
	3180	3188	3193
	3194	3198	3200
	3203	3204	4419
	4452		
MOREAU, H.	3178	3717	3845
	4294	4368	4397
	4428	4459	
MOREAU, L-A.	3754	3755	3899
	3952	3953	4433
MOREAU, L&F	3163	3168	3171
	3172	3174	3181
	3184	3185	3186
	3187	3189	3190
	3197	3201	3202
	3752	3753	
MOREAU, M.	3175	3696	3830
	4038	4185	4360
	4405	4413	4430
	4432	4450	4451
	4453	4454	4455
	4824		
MORET, A.	3322	3332	
MOREZ, V.	4293		
MORGAN, F.J.	4393		
MORIN, G.	3252	3363	3962
	4107	4108	
MORIS, L.M.	4047		
MORLON, A.	4578		
MOTZNER, V.	4330		
MOUSSON, A.	3898		
MOVIER, A.E.	3404	4693	4696
	4708		
MUCHA, ALF.	4241		
MULLER, HANS	3353	3799	3822
	4773		
MULLER, HEINZ	3289	3792	
	4158		
MULLER-C/KREFELD	3480	4231	
	4504		
MYRON	3417		
NAM GREB--BERGMAN	3572	3575	
	3602	3603	3604
	3618	3894	4377

SCULPTORS

NELSON, ALP. 4080
NELSON, ANT. 3823
NOEL, R.   4049

-O-

OBIOLS, G.   3652 3824
OMERTH, G.   3491 3675 3955
              4001 4002
OTTO, CHRIST 3310
OTTY-FURST   367A
OULINE   4579

-P-

PAGELS, H.J. 4873
PALMIER, R.   3406
PANDIANI, A.A.   3562 3563
                  3566
PANDIANI, I.A.   3561
PAPKE   3681
PARIS, R.   4012 4020 4021
PARKS, C.   3684 3685
PARSONS, E.B.   3624 3625
                  3626 3627 3628
                  3629
PASCAL, F-M. 4356
PATRISSE, A. 3732
PECHE, A.M.   3846
PEINTE, H.   4499
PELESCHKA-LONG, F.   3960
              4272
PELESCHKA-LUNARD 3840
PETSCHKE, F.H.   4242
PEVOLA   3711
PEYNOT, E.E. 3646
PHILIPPE, A.R.   4017
PHILIPS   4235
PICAULT, E-L 3160 3162 3279
              3314 3465 3477
              3478 3536 3538
              3539 3540
              3541 4046 4088
              4176 4331 4464
PICCIOLE, J.M.   3411 4304
PILET, L.   4200
PILLIG, G.   4189
PILZING, M.V.   3414
PINA, A.   3306 3308
PINEDO, E.   4860
PLACZEK, O.   3439
PLE, H.H.   4040 4041 4062
              4283 4489 4496
PLESSNER, J. 3241
POERTZEL, PROF. O.   4102
              4105 4653
POHL, A.   3873
POIRIER, H.   4204
POLLAK, J.   4058
PORRET, J.J. 4617 4618 4619
              4620 4621 4622
              4623

POZEN, V.   3546
POTTER-VONNOH, B. 4569 4571
PRADIER, J.J. 3723 4303
PRATT, G.D.   3307
PREISS, P.   4005 4006 4007
              4008 4100 4101
              4653 4668 4669
              4670 4671 4672
PRIVATE, A.G. 4588
PROCTOR, A.P. 4759
PUTNAM, B.   4194 4570
PUTTEMANS, I.D.A. 4310
PUYT, A.   4027

-R-

RAISSIGUIER, E.   3212
RANCOULET, E. 3488 4033 4324
              4325 4859
RASMUSSEN, O. 4260
REAL DEL SARTE, M. 3937
REIMANN, A.   3867
REMINGTON, F. 4756
RENDA, G.   3620
REUPER   3350
REUSCH, F.J. 3259
REVILLON, J. 3544
RHIND, J.M.   4753
RICHARD, ALF. 4028 4029
RICHER, M.L.P.   4500
RICHTER-WOLF 3365
RIEDER, J.   3649
RIESE, O.   3508
RIGUAL   3813
ROBERT, L.V.E.   4131
ROBINET, P.   4082
ROCH, R.   3737
ROCHER, G.   4608
ROLL, F.   4261
ROLLE, M.L.   3797
ROMANELLI, R. 4858
RONDONI, A.   3975
ROSSE, F.   4429
ROSSETTO, A. 4475
ROSSI, E.   4119 4271
ROUGELET, B. 3316 3317
ROUSSEAU, J. 4116
ROUX, C.A.   3444 3445
ROZET, F.   4079
RUBIN, A.   3888
RUDE, F.   350A
RUDOLFI, R.   4237
RUEL, J.   4689 4726 4727
              4728 4731 4732
RUFF, A.   3460 3731 4043
              4511 4543
RUFFONY   3492
RUISSEAU   3179

-S-

SAALMANN, E. 3283 3467

SALMSON, J.J.   3643 3798
                 4035 4036 4045
                 4046
SANZEL, F.   4406
SAULO, G.E.   4094 4095
SCARPA, G.   4281
SCHAEFER, H.   4193
SCHAFFERT   3248 3296
SCHENKEL, F.   3441
SCHIEVELKAMP, H. 3370 3372
                 3405
SCHIMMELPHFENNIG,O.   4436
SCHLIEPSTEIN, G.   4075
SCHMELENBERG   3251
SCHMIDT-CASSEL, O. 3981
SCHMIDT-FELLING   3245 3255
                 3257 3293 3295
                 3325 3326 3330
                 3334 3354 3356
                 3382 3392 3482
                 3496 351A 3671
                 4289 4536
SCHMIDT-HOFER   3215 3233 3297
                 3400 3402 3416
                 3423 3500 3505
                 3516 4249 4254
                 4255 4277 4309
SCHMIDT-KESTNER, E.   4552
SCHMIDT, N.   3959
SCHMOTZ-METZNER   3514
SCHNAUDER, R.   3254
SCHOLTER, H.   3217
SCHREINER, J-B.   4782
SCHRODEL   4819
SCHROEDTER, A.   3969
SCHWALENBERG, S.   3323 3328
                 3331 3339 3383
                 4358 4361
SECONDO   3838
SEGER, E.   3220 4279
SEGOFFIN, V.J.   4354
SEIFERT, F.   3454 4848
SEIFERT, V.H.   3342 3453 4125
                 4126 4298 4508
                 4512 4513
SIGHIERI   3821
SIGNORET-LEDIEU, L.   3726
                 4059
SOIRAM-PETERMANN, J.   3869
SOMME, T.   3800 4003 4850
SOMMER, G.   3661
SONZOWACHT, J.   4438
SOSSON, L.   3993
SPACHMAN, E.   3709
SPAMPINATO, C.   4748 4749
                 4750
SPAMPINATO, M.   4675 4676
                 4677 4678 4679
SQUELIN   4215
STEINER, C.L.   4387

STICHLING, O.   3244
STRANTZ, A. v.   3357
SZTANKO, G.   3706
                 -T-
TAVRILOV, N.Z.   3557
TELCS, M.   4796 4797
TELRIV/VERLET   3806
TERESZCZUK, P.   3687 3689
                 3879 3880 3895
                 3967 3968 3971
                 3983 4011 4015
                 4112 4201 4515
                 4517 4522
THIERMANN, P.   3377 3378 3379
                 3385
THOLENAAR, T.L.   3946
THOMAS, M.   3359
THOMASSON, E.   4540
THORWALDSEN, A.   3458
"THUSS"   3572 3575 3602
                 3603 3604 3618
                 3694 4377
TILGNER, O.V.   3477
TIMPE, F.   3425
TITO, M.   3366
TITZE, A.   4297
TOURGUENEFF, P.   4091
THYLLMANI   4165
TOBERENTZ, R.   4383
TROUBETZKOY, P.   4478
TRUPHEME, A.F.   4865
TUCH, PROF.   4210
                 -U-
UHDE, J.   4396
ULRICH, T.U.   3573 4257
UPHUES, J.   3501
                 -V-
VANNETTI, A.   4092
VARNIER, R.   4274
VAN DER STRAETEN, G. 3785 3786
                 3787 3788 3789
                 3790 3791 3826
VERLET, C.   3806 3812
VERROCCHIO   4747
VERSCHNIEDER, J.   4138 4148
                 4421
VIERTHALER, J.   4211
VIGOUREUX, P.O.   4583
VILLANIS, E.   3466 3758 3759
                 3760 3761 3762
                 3763 3764 3765
                 3766 3767 3768
                 3769 3770 3772
                 3773 3774 3775
                 3776 3777 3778
                 3779 3780 3781
                 3782 3783 3784
                 3941
VONNOH, B.P.   4569 4571

4877. CRÉPUSCULE--The Dawn and the Twilight
      By Michel Jacobs born 1877-
France. c1900. Painted Terra-Cotta. Ht: 21"
Founder Salesio, Paris.
Jacobs was born in Montreal--studied in Paris.